Canoeing
the Delaware

Pennsylvania

New York

New Jersey

Hancock
Stockport
Lordville
Long Eddy
Callicoon
Cochecton
Narrowsburg
Masthope
Westcolang Park
Lackawaxen
Sholola
Pond Eddy
Port Jervis
Milford
Montague
Dingmans Ferry
Bevans
Wallpack Center
Bushkill
Millbrook
Calno
Brotzmanville
Delaware Water Gap
Delaware Sta.
Ramsayburg
Mununka Chunk
Belvidere
Martins Creek
Foul Rift
Brainards
Easton
Phillipsburg
Carpenterville
Allentown
Riegelsville
Durham Furn.
Frenchtown
Erwinna
Tumble
Lumberville
Lambertville
Moores
Washington Crossing
Yardley
Trenton

Philadelphia

Two Hundred Miles on the Delaware River

A Canoe Cruise from Its Headwaters to the Falls at Trenton

By J. Wallace Hoff

Down the Delaware River in a Canoe

By John Boyle O'Reilly

South Jersey Culture & History Center

2025

Two Hundred Miles on the Delaware River was originally printed by The Brandt Press, Trenton, N. J., 1893. It was entered, according to Act of Congress, in the year 1893, by J. Wallace Hoff, in the Office of the Librarian of Congress, at Washington, D.C.

"Down the Delaware River in a Canoe" was printed in *Athletics and Manly Sport*, copyrighted by John Boyle O'Reilly in 1890 and published in Boston by the Pilot Publishing Company.

Both titles are republished as *Canoeing the Delaware* by the South Jersey Culture & History Center, 2025.

South Jersey Culture & History Center
Stockton University
101 Vera King Farris Drive
Galloway, NJ 08205

Additional material Copyright © 2025
ISBN: 978-1-947889-28-6

Cover photographs by Edward A. Moseley, featured in *Athletics and Manly Sport.*

A Brief Foreword

Imagine a time when modern America did not exist; a time when the Centennial celebrations of 1876 were still a fond memory. America was on the move, but not by automobile or plane. Conventional modes of travel included train, wagon, horse, or shoe leather express. For the unconventional, other choices were available and quite popular in the 1890s: bicycles and canoes.

This is not a work about bicyles. Here you will find record of two canoe trips down the Delaware River. J. Wallace Hoff and companions, members of the famed Park Island Canoeing Association of Trenton, New Jersey, voyaged from the source of the Delaware to Trenton in the autumn of 1892. John Boyle O'Reilly, famed Irish rebel (according to the press of the day) and talented poet, completed a similar trip with friends two years previously.

Both authors capture the excitement of shooting rapids (rifts in the northern section of the river), always invigorating and sometimes dangerous. The camaraderie of the canoeists is plain. These fellow travelers enjoy the company of one another. They tell inside jokes, assist one another at need, and enjoy their evenings after a hard day on the river, often around the campfire.

The star of these tales is the Delaware River itself. Hoff, O'Reilly and companions are struck by its unspoiled beauty. They often rest their paddles and drift with the current as they glide through valleys, past streams augmenting the waterway, and by mills and farms at river's edge.

They admire the scenes around them and the people they meet along the way: teamsters, fishermen, hotel keepers, canalmen and farmers. The locals are depicted with care, honorably but with their distinctive personalities on display.

If you have canoed or camped, these scenes will be familiar. If you have not, enjoy a new world that is an old world.

Hoff concludes his work with a quotation from *As You Like It*. It is a good place for this foreword to end too, though I will add the final line, which Hoff omits:

> And this our life, exempt from public haunt,
> Finds tongues in trees, books in the running brooks,
> Sermons in stones, and good in everything.
> I would not change it.

Tom Kinsella,
January 2025

Navigation

J. WALLACE HOFF

Two Hundred Miles
on the Delaware River

THE author fraternally dedicates this reminiscence of a pleasant vacation trip to those canoemen, who, when the spirit moves them, laying aside the thoughts of business for the pleasure of grasping the double blade, gladly leave behind them brick walls and the dust of towns for the eye-resting wooded hills, the clean and wholesome waterway, and the health-giving tonic of woodland odors and cool mountain breezes.

TRENTON, N. J., December 1st, 1892.

PREFACE.

T THE outset the intention of this narrative was to give a succinct account of a canoe cruise down the Delaware to enable future *voyageurs* to estimate the time required for such a trip, and also to present some of the obstacles and pleasures likely to be encountered.

We have departed from our original plan, however, because the trip was crowded with matters of interest relating to local scenery, towns and characteristic bits, so that the subject grew on our hands in a way most pleasant, at least to us, and it was natural to suppose that others would be entertained in reading about them if unable to see for themselves.

The Delaware valley proves an inexhaustible field for the artist, presenting, as it does, at every point a *vista* of landscape and background, the equal of which many among us have travelled far to see.

To the canoeist-photographer every turn brings to view an opportunity for an interesting exposure. Indeed, the temptation is to carry away so many souvenirs that one camera with its outfit hardly suffices, for—

> "The mountains that enfold
> In their wide sweep, the colored landscape round,
> Seem groups of giant kings in purple and gold
> That guard the enchanted ground."

15

The cruise requires plenty of hard work, but the result is in every way beneficial. At this day the ground can be covered without depending upon a camping outfit, as towns and villages—summer resorts—are so numerous along the line that accommodations are assured. But, I need hardly add, the only true way to thoroughly enjoy the outing is to spend the time in actual camping and cruising, recuperating the body and mind by complete change, and giving vent, if only for a short time, to the savagery, which to a greater or less degree is innate in all of us.

The autumn is the season for canoeing, and the scenery of the river country during the autumn months is glorious. Then, also, is the best bass-fishing found. Apart from the picturesque character of the section visited by us, it is also fast gaining popularity as a region for summer homes, and is dotted with towns so situated as to add variety to sport and pastime.

THE AUTHOR.

TRENTON, N. J, November 30th, 1892.

Contents.

APPENDIX 1.

A Little Bit of History.

APPENDIX 2.

Distances on the Delaware.

J. WALLACE HOFF

To the Delaware.

All powerful and restless,
On it flows to meet the ocean—
Flows the historic Delaware.
Not a jot its restless motion,
Shore, or rocks, or islets, spare.

From the heights of mountain wilds
Every spring and streamlet surges—
Rushing on in glee to swell,
By its force, the changing dirges
Of the mighty river's spell.

As th' untutored child of Nature,
Strong its arm, as sure and swift,
Down its rock-barred courses wild
Forms it here an isle or rift:
Yet at times 'tis peaceful, mild.

EN PASSANT.

Countless ages gone, and coming:
Roll'st thou as in days of yore?
Or, whilst in thine angry spite,
Hast thou a deep valley wore,
Ribbed and scoréd by thy might ?

Still thou floweth on, resistless,
Flowing in, and out, and onward,
Ever gaining strength and force
As the fall, which, rushing downward,
Swells thy torrent in its course.

J. WALLACE HOFF

CHAPTER 1.

A Trenton Conoeing Picture.
Camping and Cruising Discussed.
The Route Mapped.
Personnel and Matériel.

J. WALLACE HOFF

> I hear the babbling to the vale
> > Of sunshine and of flowers,
> But unto me thou bring'st a tale
> > Of visionary hours.—*Wordsworth.*

BEAUTIFUL moonlight evening in the month of July, during the year 1891. In one corner of the broad porch at the front of a group of canoe-houses overlooking the Delaware river, at Trenton, N. J., sit two members of the Park Island Canoeing Association engaged in earnest conversation. Around them is bustle and confusion: canoeists with paddles and pipes, sails and canoes are passing and repassing from the floats to the houses, whilst canoes are lying along-shore or darting across or up river. In front of one of the houses two of the graceful craft are being packed for a camp at Park Island. In the club-houses, lights and lanterns shed their brilliancy, disclosing racks of canoes, duffle, paddles, and other articles whose value is so well known to the canoeing fraternity. Close to the "Colony" flows the waveless river, its swift current scarcely heard save where it sweeps past some entangled bush or exposed rock.

In the distance can be heard the ceaseless surging of the Trenton Falls.

The animated picture was one of nightly occurrence to the canoemen mentioned, and was just the condition of things to direct the thoughts into canoeing channels.

The two members before mentioned were discussing at this moment, between clouds of fragrant smoke, their annual vacation. That it would be in some way connected with canoeing and camping was assured. But how? Would it be a camp at "Rum-brag,"* Eagle Island, the Millstone, at Park Island, or would it be *a cruise?*

Camps are all well enough in their way, but the idea was given up immediately when the last proposition was advanced. The suggestion was met with such enthusiasm that at a later hour, when lights were out and silence reigned supreme, two blanket-enwrapped canoeists tossed uneasily upon their cots, troubled by visions of swift currents and foam-lashed falls, with which they were battling in a journey down the Delaware from its headwaters to the tide.

The romantic moon was responsible for a realistic undertaking.

The proposed cruise soon became noised about, and within a week the party was increased to six canoeists, and the date of starting fixed for September the twelfth. The personnel and matériel of the trip were as follows:

William M. Carter, canoe *Zerlina*, 15x30,** Peterboro canoe, full-decked, with six foot pointed cockpit and canvas cover.

Clark Cooper, canoe *Nyleptha*, 15x30, Clinker built, by Wiser, of Philadelphia, full-decked, oval cockpit, with cover, with fore and aft compartments for dry stowage.

Harry Allen, canoe *Werowance,* 12x26, Watertown Canoe company, smooth skin. This was originally an open

---

* A fishing camp on the Delaware.
** These measurements, as presented in the original text, appear to describe canoe length in feet and beam, the widest breadth, in inches, thus 15 feet x 30 inches. The *Nahiwi* also, apparently, includes depth at 10 inches.

boat, but had been decked to meet the requirements of the trip. Although the smallest of the fleet, she was very dry.

Frederick Donnelly, 15x30, Bowdish canoe, smooth skin, curved stem and stern-posts. A very pretty open canoe, entirely covered with oiled drilling.

The author, canoe *Nahiwi*, 14x30x10, an open Watertown hunting canoe, smooth skin, covered with oiled canvas. This canoe was the first open canoe paddled on the Delaware at Trenton, and weighs about fifty-five pounds.

The balance of our equipments consisted of canoe traps, camp blankets, tents, cots, cooking utensils, skeleton stoves and oil stoves, provision kits, lanterns, hatchets and toilet bags.

The sporting outfit comprised an Anthony and a Hawkeye plate camera, fishing implements and a pistol. This outfit, we are sorry to say, reached port in bad condition, the Hawkeye being warped and swollen out of its fine elegant joints, warranted perfectly light-proof; the fishing tackle devoid of glittering spoons and bloated rubber minnows and minus from ten to fifty feet of its original length, and the pistol—well, a little Stockport dew soon rendered the breech more dangerous than the muzzle, and made a self-cocking, rapid-firing self-ejector as harmless as some cannon of General Washington's, with which we are all familiar.

CHAPTER 2.

These Canoeists in General.
Some Asides.
From Trenton to Hancock.
Towns and Scenery.
Port Jervis.
Glimpses of the River.
John Boyle O'Reilly.
Afloat on the Headwaters of The Delaware.
The First Night's Camp.

Up with my tent; here will I lie to-night,
But where to-morrow? Well, all's one for that.
—*Richard III*

OR punctuality and dependence (and indepen-dence, too) commend to me a canoeist. If he says he will do a thing, he'll do it, and at the time agreed upon. "If he says he won't, he won't, you may depend upon it."

Our only roll call was the week previous to our start, when we shipped canoes and outfits. At that time the fell hand of death necessitated the withdrawal from our party of one whom we all counted on having with us. Sorrowing with him in his loss, we accepted the situation, making up by keeping our absent comrade apprised of our movements and experiences as best we could.

It was at 5:15 o'clock on a Saturday morning that four of our party gathered at the station, equipped for the all-rail journey to Hancock, N. Y., free mortals for ten whole days and a distance of four hundred and twenty-five miles. The morning was gray and the crowd looked sleepy. Exchang-ing confidences, each confessed to having resorted to the fiendish alarm-clock in order to be on time. And one, Oh, horrors! despairing of the "rouseful" abilities of one clock owned up to having impressed two into service. Cab orders were filled as usual, one man being served at 4:30, another forgotten entirely. At 5:37 the Pittsburgh train came rolling in, and we began the first stage of the journey, to Jersey

City. We made good time, and as the morning advanced introduced into our apartment some fresh air for the sleepy passengers to digest. The discussion of railroad and river maps occupied a great deal of attention, for, with one exception, we were entirely unacquainted with the country through which we were to cruise. Tiring of this, we took up the discussion of fruit and sandwiches furnished by "my wife's mother-in-law," finally drifting into speculations concerning some of our feminine fellow-travelers.

One brunette, with tumbled hair and bedraggled costume, we sat down as an "all-nighter." She braced up as the day advanced, and got out at Newark. Of two others—one a pretty blonde with an elegant figure, the other a brune-blonde, petite and pleasant-faced, we decided were sisters, evidently traveling in a new country, as they occupied single seats near the windows, and kept up an incessant conversation. We concluded that they had gotten on at some station down the road—Philadelphia, probably, as they carried bouquets of fresh lowers, and had clean complexions.

For the sake of accuracy, and the benefit of whom it may concern, I will explain that during the foregoing study and deductions, Carter was asleep in the forward part of the car.

We caught glimpses of New Brunswick, Metuchen, Iselin, Rahway, Linden, Newark, and Jersey City, all bathed in the early morning sun.

The latter place we reached at 7:35, and ran into the ferry over the recently completed elevated tracks of the Pennsylvania company, catching bits of early morning domesticity through fluttering curtains and half-closed blinds, characteristic of second-story boudoir and dining-room living.

Imagine this parade of household affairs, ye retired country-dwellers and would-be-secluded city tenants.

We ran into the new arched terminal station of the Pennsylvania railroad, with its amazing network of iron and wire-rope girders and stays, its interior flooded with light through the immense lights in the roof stretching from end to end. This is the largest railroad station in the world, not even excepting that of St. Pancras. It covers four acres of ground, is 652 feet long, 256 feet wide and 115 feet high.

Another innovation, the double-decked ferry-boat, we missed, as the intended second-story waiting-room was not completed. Going down a flight of steps we took the regulation boat for New York.

The trip through the city up to the Chambers street ferry by way of the water-front at this early hour gave us a little insight into several novelties. We passed fish-stalls, poultry booths, cheap restaurants and sidewalk "stores"— under awnings and in cellars. From the typical groggery, ambled down-at-the-heel and blear-eyed roustabouts, wiping away the burning spray after a nip of questionable character, bought with some chance coin picked up the day before.

On one hand a "hatter" with a sparsely-splinted whisk flicked spots of dust from antiquated tiles, felts and straws. Further on a couple of fat cooks, complacently seated on peach baskets along the curb, jabbed their thumbs and fore-fingers into the weather indicators of skinny-looking chickens, much to the disgust of the merchants.

At our heels hung three "job hunters," one of whom in choice dialect advised his companion to strike out for the country in search of work. Said he, "Ever buddy is 'er makin' fer der big towns an' doan giv' a feller no chance,

See?"—a bit of philosophy his friends readily seconded, showing that if one-half of the world does not know how the other half lives, it can make a pretty shrewd guess.

Jostling through the motley throng we embarked on a screw ferry-boat, the ample, clean cabin-room of which we all remarked, and in a few minutes landed at the New York, Lake Erie and Western railroad station. We were again in Jersey City.

In explanation of our round-about route, I would state it was at the suggestion of Clark whose object in going over to New York was to avoid the crowds, and attendant delay to be met with in Jersey City. As our guide is a thorough Jerseyman, I leave further consideration of the subject with the reader.

Securing tickets, guide-books, morning papers and other reading matter, we repaired to the dining-room, where, seating ourselves at the round table, we ordered a hungry man's breakfast. We had been canoeing all summer, and there was not an impaired digestion in the crowd.

While we were loitering over coffee, Fred tumbled in on us, fresh from an evening and morning in New York. Of course, his experiences were manifold.

Later we learned that these experiences were the result of a triple-expansion, high-pressure imagination, and we found a safe average was one-third of his results. For example, some of his two-feet bass, which always succeeded in escaping as they were being hauled into the canoe, might be reduced to eight inches.

At 9:20 we boarded the Erie vestibule, and were soon *en route* for Hancock. Counting noses, we found our force as follows: Carter, the "father" (later contracted to "Dad") of the expedition, so called on account of age and experience, and from the fact that the trip we were about to make was made by him in 1882; Cooper, the Association's traveler, bicyclist, canoeist, photographer, and CRANK; Allen, amateur canoeist, photographer and botanist; Donnelly (the quartermaster), a recruit to the ranks of canoemen and cruisers, who turned out the crowd's tonic by day and by night in a double sense, besides being a general informer on topics of interest—with the usual proviso; lastly, the logkeeper, the title sufficing in this direction.

We had over a hundred and sixty miles to go and then our troubles, like those of the little bears, would begin. But miles and troubles are as naught in these days, and, besides, we were traveling through a country abounding in excellent scenery. The Ramapo and Delaware valleys and the Delaware Highlands certainly justify the admiration bestowed upon them. The scenery is a constant panoramic change. 'Neath precipitous hills we rush to cosy villages and busy towns, and then on to stretches of level country devoted to fruit and stock-raising. The rural surroundings, health-giving atmosphere, and glimpses of long, low farmhouses, suggesting peaceful comforts amidst a land of plenty, cause the city resident to sigh for the things he enjoyeth not.

> "Oh! friendly to the best pursuits of man.
> Friendly to thought, to virtue, and to peace.
> Domestic life in rural pleasures past!"

From Jersey City to Mahwah the road runs in and out of the famous country drained by the Passaic river. Rutherford, Garfield, Passaic, Clifton, Paterson, Ridgewood, Hohokus and Ramsey's, with from six hundred to fifteen thousand population, are some of the well-known towns through which we pass.

The first town across the New Jersey line is Suffern. The rest of our journey was through rocky defiles and fertile plains in New York state. Quoting from the Erie guide-book, the surroundings are described as follows:

"At Suffern the Erie swings into the Ramapo valley, through a narrow defile. For fifteen miles the valley extends, mountain bound, and at times is of barely sufficient width to allow the passage, side by side, of the river, the historic post-road and the Erie; while again it will widen out in a dell or ravine which marks the course of a mountain rill or torrent. Here and there, too, the mountains recede, and the valley spreads itself into a fertile plain, and in these occasional plateaus nestle, in the order named, the little hamlets of Hillburn, Ramapo, Sterlington, Sloatsburg, Tuxedo Park (with its hard driving roads, picturesque stone fences and lodge-house at the entrance to well-kept estates), Southfields and Arden. The river is a panorama of rare beauty. Its head-waters are in a series of mountain springs and lakes, and in its course through the valley it first meanders across the flat lands, then sinks into a narrow deep bowl, to widen presently into a placid lake, and finally, before its exit into the level country beyond the valley, it tumbles over a ledge of rocks, and falls, a seething, roaring mass, to its rocky bed fully fifty feet below. In the quiet portions the boating is charming; the banks now and then open into snug grottoes and dells, down which come sparkling, splashing streams from the rock-bound springs above, while the dense overhanging foliage affords a refreshing shade, and there are many sheltered pools where the bathing is delightful. The river, as well as the mountain lakes from which it springs, is populous with game-fish, and in the wooded mountains small game of every variety is plentiful, insuring to the visitor the best sport with gun and rod."

And what is said of this spot is equally true of other localities in this section and beyond. At every turn mountain and lowland vistas, bold knobs and deep gullies broke upon the view.

At Turners, where a short stop was made to await the New York express, the boys went to sample the famous Orange county milk on tap at the railroad restaurant. They all agreed as to its excellence, and Carter sighed for a bottle.

All aboard! The journey is resumed, and we fly past Monroe, Oxford, Greycourt, Chester, Goshen, Hampton, Middletown (where the rasping pun, How do you make Moses from the word Middletown? Ans. Leave off "iddletown" and add "oses" was sprung as usual), Howells, Otisville, Guymard—all in Orange county—and at 12:30 we reach Port Jervis.

Heavens and earth, boys, what's the racket? Bees? No wonder the question. The air resounds with the pandemonium and clatter so well known to bee-keepers on a swarm day. Out on the platform all is bustle and confusion. Pretty maidens with their elderly mammas, or chaperones, parade about, laden with shawls, grips and boxes awaiting the making up of the new train. Trucks, trunks and milk cans lie all about the station. Stage drivers and hotel runners jostle and squeeze, swear and coax.

"Refreshments."

In front of the inviting hotel doorway and around it a sable son of Senegambia rubbles a puncher on the disk of a brass plate in suspension, calling you in this polite way "to dinnah!" For once, where there is noise there is comfort. Going into the long building on the left, the crowd hustles us to the lunch counter, where boot-legs of milk and pyramids of sandwiches and pie, cups of coffee and plates of cake greet the eye. No traditional railroad lunch here. Everything is sweet and clean, and we have unlimited time.

We were soon on the road again. From Port Jervis the railroad winds along the river bank, and we watched the rifts and falls with feverish anxiety whenever close enough, speculating on our chances of a safe journey home. The river had been falling for the past week, and some rifts were dangerously low. Others again were deep and rocky, and visions of swamped and broken boats, and duffle afloat to the sea filled our imaginations.

Hancock at 3:20 P. M.

Grasping paddles and bundles, we left the stuffy car for a breath of fresh air and a sight of the East Branch. We found the town rather a dusty place among the hills, situated in what was formerly known as Hardenburg's Patent. It has three large hotels, several groceries, a hardware store, newspaper office, etc.

We went at once to the freight station to look up canoes and dunnage. The little God of Luck was with us. We found everything as shipped from Trenton, but could not help expostulating at the manner in which the canoes were piled—light and empty ones at the bottom and the heavy, loaded ones on top—a state of things favoring a bad strain or a tear in cockpit hatches and covers. The agent, who was obliging, and assisted us in every way possible, explained that the boats had only arrived that morning.

We had shipped them the week previous and shrugged our shoulders at the close connection.

Talk about a boy with his first gun, or a girl with a new beau. The sights around us made all anxious for an immediate start. All but the novice. He thought it a good plan to stop over night at a hotel and make an early start in the morning.

Well!

Allen was picking cinders out of his eyes, Carter gasping for breath, and the rest with throats like salamanders, and here was a would-be canoeist preferring a stuffy hotel to a woodland camp.

As a punishment we deputized him in his capacity as Quartermaster to see to the purchase of provisions, while the rest, hunting up a couple of carts, soon had canoes and dunnage at the water's edge.

The *Nahiwi*, first to kiss the waters of the East branch, was drawn up alongside a heavy scow, into which I had transferred most of my duffle.

Just before packing, an elderly gentlemen in the crowd was so enthused with the canoes as they lay bunched on the shore, and with the idea of a cruise, that he asked permission to try one of the canoes. Upon my placing my canoe at his disposal he jumped in, and, preferring a single blade, gracefully paddled across the river and up a swift rift, returning out of breath with the unusual exercise. We were agreeably surprised at his steady seat, for although he stated that he was used to boats, a sixty-pound open canoe with ten-inch siding is not steady riding.

At the foot of Point Mountain, in a deep pool just below a small rift that dashes under the iron bridge, we packed our impedimenta. The usual crowd of curious natives gazed upon the operation from a respectful distance. The canoes of the veterans, through constant practice on many camps and cruises of by-gone days, were stowed and trimmed with precision each morning, and methodically unpacked to expedite the making of each night's camp. We knew from experience the necessity of careful trimming and the danger, while running a rapid, of a badly-balanced boat, or one down in the nose.

As for the Quartermaster, he learned a great many wrinkles conducive to comfort in canoeing before we struck our last camp. In my opinion the most important was that a square tin bread canister is at no time more noticeable than when stowed abaft the forward thwart, within reach of the knees of a long-legged canoeist.

The Mohawk, or West branch of the Delaware river, rises in the Catskill mountain range, in Schoharie county, New York; the Popacton (Popacktunk O. S.), or East branch, in the mountain fastnesses of Greene and Ulster counties. Both branches flow through a thinly-settled country, wild and lonesome in the extreme. They are separated by lofty mountain ranges, and, running nearly parallel, meet a short distance below Hancock, at the base of Point Mountain, a name whose appropriateness will be seen when compared with the photograph, which shows plainly its distinctive feature. Both streams are supplied by numerous kills, large and small, some being named on the maps in the Indian and Dutch tongues, but a larger number bearing no name at all.

The Popacton is very shallow from Arkville to Hancock. Mr. Carter, with two Trenton canoeists, Messrs. Frank Sigler and R. G. Lucas, of the Crescent Canoe Club, made the trip in 1882, during the month of June, and had hard canoeing. Although they had a rafting "fresh," the shallows gave them considerable annoyance.

The same year, later in the season, two New York canoeists attempted the trip, and had to give it up on account of the low stage of the water. In 1885, John Boyle O'Reilly, at that time flush with triumphs from pen and paddle, in company with three comrades, essayed the trip from Hancock. They found the water so low that they were compelled to re-ship their fleet to Port Jervis, from whence they made a new start. Mr. O'Reilly's article in the December, 1886, issue of the *Boston Pilot* had been read by each of us, and our familiarity with this and his other works gave occasion to frequent references to the gentlemanly advocate of out-of-door culture. A feeling of sympathy arose for the time being, strengthened doubtless by the fact that our thoughts and craft, although at different periods, were running in the same channels. In common with thousands of others, Trenton canoemen heard with deep sorrow the story of his sudden end; the testimony from all was that at the close, as in the high noon of his life, he was truly noble.

At 4:30 P. M. we passed the word "Ready!" Cooper and Allen shot their cameras at the scenery, the crowd, and the loaded and manned canoes, and we pushed out into the East branch, two hundred miles from home, one thousand feet above the sea level, and surrounded by towering mountains and cliffs, which were rapidly shutting out the sun's warm rays.

Ye Gods of health and strength! to you we drank the cheer we felt, in deepest draughts of pure, fresh mountain air, swept from hills of spruce and pine, filtered through branches and cooled by deep ravine and rocky gorge. We drank to you in cups of clean—yes, *clean*,—wholesome water, dipped over the canoe's side from a mountain stream fed by countless springs, cool, deep and swift. No pollution here; its cleanliness you could both see and taste.

In our enjoyment of the scene around us, we made the mountains ring with our overflowing spirits. As we skirted the base of the mountain, in comparatively deep water, Cooper and Carter were suddenly "hung up" on partly submerged rocks, twisting about on keels just amidships. They were gotten off without trouble, but we had the laugh on them.

We found the East branch shallow and narrow. Just below the town we struck our first rift. The choppy ripples in the swift shoot lapped playfully the bows of our buoyant craft, giving the stern a parting dash as we left the last rush in our wake. After that, shallows and rifts being of such common occurrence, we gave them no especial thought, unless to wish for their aid when we were in some long, smooth stretch or eddy, through which it meant work to paddle. At the end of Point Mountain, which was reached in a short time, we met the waters of the Mohawk branch. At the conjunction of the streams we found a large raft stranded. This diverted the channel, and both tributaries entered the larger river—the Delaware proper—with a musical rush, as though glad to cease their checkered course in their own shallow beds.

It was well we started from Hancock. Further up we should have experienced great trouble, even if we had the great good fortune of getting through at all.

The West branch is well named, for, as we cast our eyes up its course, indicated by winding mountains as far as eye could see, the setting sun bathed our polished craft in a flood of golden light, tinting the waters ahead and behind, and bathing with his rays the far reaching Highlands. Getting a photographic view of the landscape, we resumed paddling, having started in earnest on our voyage down the Delaware.

Rips and raps were of frequent occurrence. If deep enough we floated through them. If we lost the channel, which was often the case, we stepped overboard and guided and hauled the canoes over the gravelly bottom to deeper water. This was not scientific canoeing, but it saved time.

Donnelly trolled, and had several strikes, getting a couple of fine bass and losing one or two at the head of rifts. Then came a quiet paddle, during which with some trouble we found a camp site just below Stockport, and at 6:20 pitched tents and started fires.

The ground was stony, and tent pegs would barely hold, so we pegged the tents down with rocks to our entire satisfaction. After this experience, we agreed to hunt for a camping ground earlier, as darkness soon pervaded the valley, when the sun's rays left it.

This, our first camp of the trip, comprised three tents, Cooper and the author together, up stream, Carter and Allen next, and then Donnelly, who was going it on the individual plan. He received during the trip all sorts of advice and help, and, for the purpose of keeping even, paid each one back to the best of his ability.

There was also lots of fun at the novice's camping and cooking, but the meal was ready at last, and so, down between deep hills, in gathering darkness and quietness, surrounded by forests, rocks and stream, we ate our suppers with wholesome relish.

We had had some wading to do—but the water was warm and we had paid no attention to our wettings. We dried our clothes before a big fire that sent smoke and flames and sparks skyward; we smoked, swapped fish stories, and watched the reflection of the moon over the mountain tops, the stars, and snaky streams of light from passing trains on the opposite bank. At last, at 9:30 P. M., we turned in to sleep in our first bivouac at the foot of the mountains of the Delaware Highlands.

CHAPTER 3.

Mountain Mists.
Rifts.
Cruising Rules.
Description of Saw Mill.
The Peculiarities of the Delaware.
Black Bass.
Lordville.
Paradise Pool.
A Lumber Shute.
Long Eddy.
Log Booms and Ferry Boats.
Dinner at Armstrong's.
A Little Chemistry.
Camping in a Thunder-Storm.

The turf shall be my fragrant shrine,
My temple, Lord! that arch of thine;
My censers breath the mountain airs,
And silent thoughts my only prayers.—*Moore*.

SUNDAY.

The previous evening had been quite warm, but towards morning the atmosphere became cold and penetrating and we wrapped ourselves closer in the warm blankets.

We awakened at seven o'clock, three of us, at least, having had a fine night's sleep. Carter had not been feeling well, and consequently slept lightly. Allen also was sick during the night, and what with pain and dosing, did not get over the effects until some hours after rising.

Upon looking out of the tents, we found the heavy night mist hanging over the valley and dripping from bushes and trees. The greensward glistened with bead-like drops, and from the rocks that hung over the stream the condensed vapor slowly trickled to some angle, whence it fell with musical tinkle. During our trip we found that this heavy mist prevailed every morning until we reached Ramsaysburg, N. J., one hundred and twenty-five miles down river, where the valley begins to widen and the low rolling lands appear. The dampness was dispelled by the sun as soon as its rays could strike in over the mountain tops, which, however, was not until about eight o'clock. This made a late morning for us.

By the time we had our breakfast over, it became very warm, the vapor acting as a burning glass to collect the heat.

On this morning we were in no particular hurry. The early hours gave promise of a pleasant day, and we had many things of interest to occupy our attention. By the time we were ready to pack, the sun had thoroughly dried our tents and clothing.

At last we pushed away from camp, drifting slowly into the current, which at the first bend carried us into a rift. Indeed, a noticeable fact in our cruise was that every camp, with one exception, was made above a rift or fall. We thus each day had an early reminder of the work before us.

Knowing that we had some hard work ahead before the trip would be finished, and not being hardened to the continuous use of the blades, we did not exert ourselves, merely paddling a trifle faster than the current. To-day, too, we not only had a couple in our party somewhat indisposed, but Donnelly was considered a novitiate to be broken in without being broken up. To accomplish with pleasure two hundred miles in canoes, sitting steadily and wielding even a light paddle, requires a gradual prelimi-nary hardening.

By following our plan as above, when we rounded to under the bluff at our island home each man found himself benefitted and rested, and although we paddled only twelve miles the first day, forty-four were logged on the last.

Just below our camp, in a bend and facing a smooth lake-like opening in the Highlands, we found hidden away one of the numerous saw mills to be met with in this section. From its location and characteristics it was worth photographing, and Cooper brought his camera into play. Paddling across stream, and running the canoe alongside of a group of up-river punts, I went ashore to inspect. I found the mill was used for sawing heavy logs into planking. The logs were hauled from the mountain-side lumber districts by teams, or in season floated down stream. The buildings, three in number, for sheltering workmen and machinery, were erected in what had been a mountain gully. The possibility of a washout was prevented by a stout dam of earth and timbers, braced by rocks, built above. This dam stopped in its course a tiny mountain rivulet, whose channel, diverted from its bed higher up, was led around to the right by a circuitous route and then carried *over* its natural bed, and thirty feet above it, by means of a trestle-supported wooden shute, to a log flume, four feet square, into which the water tumbled, operating an overshot wheel. Huge piles of sawdust and lumber scraps lay scattered about. This *debris* is annually cleared away by the large freshets, the water necessarily rising high in the narrow valley.

The inspection over, and the photograph taken, we resumed paddles. The river twisted and turned continually, and at every bend we encountered a shallow rift with an accompanying eddy.

Before leaving the mountain chains, an interesting peculiarity in the course of the stream was often pressed upon our notice. Looking ahead of us, we would imagine from the formation of the ranges that our way was always to the right of the bend. But in many instances we were badly deceived. In fact, there was no telling how the channel would bear, as a small underlying mountain, or a level stretch, would cause an entirely new formation, and it would be hours before we would reach that portion of the course reckoned upon. Of course, the aggregate of these bends made our mileage one and a half times greater than if we had traveled in a straight line.

It was a perfect September morning, with cloudless sky and warm sun, and scarcely a disturbance on the water's surface, save where it passed over a partly sunken rock, or rushed down a steep incline.

Carter, Allen and Donnelly trolled, catching ten or twelve very fine black bass. We were traveling almost too fast for successful fishing. Several spoons were lost, and points of hooks were continually broken as the canoes floated over shallow, rocky rips.

About twelve o'clock we coasted down a steep rift, and landed under the bridge at Lordville. Very appropriately the names of the day and the place coincided. For us the place proved lucky also, as several very necessary things were accomplished. Not the least of these was the use of the post office and telegraph station, at which latter place Allen wired home for a pair of stout blades to be sent to him at Port Jervis, as he had broken his light spoon blades early in the morning.

The custodian at the toll bridge was a very interesting elderly man, witty and full of life. He was well informed on the topics of the day, and kept up a newsy conversation until we left.

Under the bridge the current ran swift and clear, and we floated for a long distance, watching the quickly disappearing stones and shells on the bottom as we rushed over them.

About two o'clock we shot down a rift, the foot of which seemed to run under a mountain, the largest and most beautiful in point of shape and evergreen growth that we had yet seen.

Suddenly, making an elbow bend, we glided into a deep, placid pool. That it was deep we knew from the impossibility of touching bottom with an eleven foot paddle although it was darted downward with force enough to cause it to disappear from sight. That it was placid the want of a single disturbing ripple, even to the next bend, denoted. We were shut in by mountains; we were mere specks in the midst of nature's grandeur.

Receding from the sharp bend, westerly, the elevations and depressions as far as eye could reach showed a pleasing picture of sunlight and shadow fantastically broken and controlled by the ranges of hills. The Pennsylvania side of the river was thickly studded with ponderous half-submerged rocks. These rocks were curiously formed of layers of limestone, cemented, seemingly, one above another, and worn smooth and round by the action of ice and water.

The solitude and peaceful surroundings made a little paradise in which we were prone to tarry awhile, but we must onward, so, making a material impression on the dry-plate, we dropped down stream, recalling the words from Bryant's hymn.

> "My heart is awed within me when I think
> Of the great miracle that still goes on,
> In silence round me—the perpetual work
> Of thy creation, finished, yet renewed
> Forever."

Some distance above Long Eddy we came to a lumber slide, built down the mountain side from the plateau above.

To inspect it, I ran my canoe behind a large rock and landed. Looking upward, I saw, disappearing in the thick growth almost straight above me, a narrow opening, made by cutting away trees and underbrush. About fifty feet from the river, in the center of the opening, a mighty hickory tree, trimmed some twenty-five feet from the ground, had been left standing. This sturdy tree supported, far better than artificial braces, the end of a V-shaped shute of hemlock, the beginning of which was out of sight among the trees. The logs, being cut and trimmed in the forests above, are placed in the shute and started down. Gathering momentum as they proceed, they slide to the end of the trough, when they shoot viciously into space and then drop into the river. This vigorous friction wears the shute as smooth as glass.

I made the ascent to the top, a feat that required a great deal of wind and grip, and gave Cooper a chance to catch a snap shot at a log as it launched into the air. The descent to the water's edge was made zig-zag fashion, with several missteps and slides which happily were not serious.

Afloat again, we were compelled to go outside a small boom, held out from shore by anchoring in mid stream, and built to catch the logs as they came floating down. From this boom they are pushed into the current again, only to be caught and shunted over to the New York shore by a big boom, stretching entirely across the stream at Long Eddy.

We lifted over the log boom and held a council close by a ferry boat peculiar to the section, and used to connect the shore ends of the main highways in New York and Pennsylvania.

These ferry boats we met with all along the river. Some are run diagonally across stream, guided by trolley and guys, and propelled by iron-shod punting or setting poles, or huge, cumbersome oars. Others are reeled across by a windlass, to which a submerged cotton or wire rope is attached. The boats are about twenty-five feet in length, ten feet beam, with sides two feet high. The ends are built alike, each being merely a continuation of the bottom above the load line on an incline, and extending past the siding. This forms a gang-way to the road, enabling teams to be driven on board from one end and on land from the other.

Our council was for the purpose of discussing whether we should or should not stop for dinner. We were all hungry, and had been having plenty of exercise. Besides, the clouds we had noticed early in the afternoon were becoming darker, and ominous thunder mutterings sounded among the Highlands. As if to decide us a few drops of rain came pattering down.

Yes, we would try for a meal at Charles Armstrong's Maple Grove Hotel, at which place, a man with a kettle informed us, we could get a "square meal."

Fastening down the canvas covers and donning oilskins we tramped up to the hotel, sun-burned and wet. Donnelly had gone ahead to order the meal, and, as it was late, he reported that we would have to take what was set before us. Having had previous experience at country boarding-houses we acquiesced, being sure of plenty to eat. While waiting, we engaged in conversation with a Mr. Rose, whom we found to be Mr. Armstrong's right-hand man in his numerous enterprises.

Mr. Rose asked us if we had time to inspect a native industry—refining wood. Noting that we looked at him quizzically, he said, " Yes, that's what I mean—to be more accurate—manufacturing wood alcohol."

At this remark Allen, who had handled the product in the hardware business, nodded his head, and said it would be worth seeing.

Under the guidance of Mr. Rose, we went a short distance down the main street, and turned into the factory yard.

On the opposite side of the street, in a vacant lot, we saw innumerable piles of cord-wood. Here was the secret of the lumber slide on the mountain and the log-boom.

In the yard, under long sheds, were heaps of charcoal. In an open court were rows of iron vats, from under the lids of which steam with a strong odor was issuing. Entering the building, we saw before us eight furnaces with high iron retorts above them. The retorts were full of wood, and in the furnaces the hottest of charcoal fires.

The stench that pervaded the place was awful—a combination of charcoal gas—sweet smelling and over-powering, alcohol and tar.

Going back of the furnaces we found high wooden tanks filled with clear cold water from a mountain stream nearby, through which ran coiled pipes, connecting with the retorts and with a large pipe at the foot of the tanks, which latter pipe ran to a sunken vat. Further on in the store-room were heaps of acetate of lime, and vats of crude alcohol and wood-tar. The process of extracting these products, as explained to us, was as follows:

The cord wood is stacked in the retorts, above the furnaces, and allowed to carbonize as in the making of charcoal in southern New Jersey. But the details of the process are different. Here all the gas, smoke and steam generated from the hard wood, instead of being wasted, is carried by tubes from the retorts into a huge vat. The pipes running through the cold water, as before stated, causes the condensation of a compound of lime, alcohol, tar and pyroligneous acid—the latter being a crude commercial form of acetic acid. The quicker the distillation the freer from impurities is the latter product.

The alcohol (pyroxylic, or wood spirit,) is a cheap grade, smelling of smoke and tar, and is distilled at a high grade of temperature from the chloride of calcium, the other products being separated at a temperature below boiling point.

The alcohol when refined has lost the odors which it had at first, so that it may be used in the manufacture of cheap perfumery. Its principal use, however, is in making varnishes.

A fair grade of gas is obtained, and is used in this case to illuminate the factory, which is running the year around, save when it is necessary to stop for repairs. The tar is insoluble and holds the more solid particles in suspension. It is used for protecting fence posts and the exposed ends of timbers.

All the products are salable commodities. The alcohol brings sixty-five cents per gallon wholesale; the charcoal brings fifteen cents per bushel, and is also used in the furnaces; the tar has a limited sale. A cord of wood, costing two dollars delivered, will produce forty bushels of charcoal and twenty gallons of alcohol.

By the time our lecture and sight-seeing was finished, dinner was announced, and we turned from chemistry to cookery.

The *menu* plainly in sight was: Cold roast beef, ham, eggs, pickled cucumbers, brown bread, wheat bread, crackers, apple sauce, ice cream and pie. You ran no risk of hearing "we're just out, very sorry," provided you ordered from the board. It took us an hour to do justice to the viands, and the sick ones, sick no longer, performed wonders in the eating line. Allen even committed the indiscretion of eating two plates of cream.

Our waitress discovered herself to be a city-bred damsel from her want of knowledge of the locality and the condition of the river, as compared with other seasons. It would not do to overlook her noticeable graciousness toward the Quartermaster, who had honeyed her into getting ready for us, notwithstanding the fact that she was dressed for an outing.

During the meal the captain of the *Nahiwi* called for a plain, common every-day knife. This request is not to be understood as disparaging the ham, although the knife he was using—a plated affair—was the wrong tool for the work in hand. On finishing, he remarked that he was afraid to eat very heartily as it interfered with paddling. Cooper, looking at him, cynically inquired, "Great Scott! What do you call a hearty meal? I'd like to know."

We decided to reel off a few more miles before camping, and a little after four o'clock we bade goodbye to the genial James and to Long Eddy and started off in a thunder shower, the heavy clashes reverberating from peak to peak as they passed down the valley.

Just below the town we ran the worst rift of the day, all being hung up with the exception of Carter. Consequently, four of us were soaking wet. At half-past five o'clock we found ourselves a short distance above Callicoon, and, the rain having partially ceased, we halted at a pretty knoll on the Pennsylvania bank, and soon had our tents pitched under the trees. We had hardly finished pegging down when the rain commenced to pour down in torrents. Changing to dry clothes we were soon reading, writing, smoking and discussing the events of the day. At 10:30, sun-burned and sleepy, we "doused the glim," glad to rest after a day of pleasant experiences.

As the least downfall of rain has a marked effect on the narrow river, we tied our boats securely, hoping for higher water and an easier passage.

CHAPTER 4.

Amenities.
Hints.
Scenery.
Cochecton Falls.
Fatigues of Portage.
A Ruined Habitation.
Narrowsburg.
Hotel Arlington.
Big Eddy.

> There was a roaring in the wind all night;
> The rain came heavily and fell in floods;
> But now the sun is rising, calm and bright;
> The birds are singing in the distant woods.—*Wordsworth.*

"DO YOU fellows expect to get up to-day?" Thus were Cooper and I awakened by Donnelly at a little after six o'clock. "I don't care whether I do or not, as I am perfectly comfortable," answered my tent mate.

In throwing down the coverlet my hand came in contact with the canvas, soaked with moisture. "Ugh!" I exclaimed, and again snuggled under the warm blankets.

A misty morning was bad enough, but a misty morning after a rainy night? 'Twas a consummation not to be devoutly wished.

In front of the camp Allen was trying to build a fire with wet wood, and I expected him to say he was smoking out a swarm of mosquitoes. But he didn't.

He simply looked anguish through a pair of watered optics.

Someone whispered "kerosene."

Chug. Chug. Up ran a blaze, and the lard in the pan was boiling in the time you are reading this paragraph.

Carter was cleaning fish down by the water's edge. Donnelly was wrestling with dish washing.

Such industrious examples must be heeded. Turning back the flaps of the tent, Cooper and I sunned ourselves a minute and then turned out. Something was wrong with us. We felt strange. What was wanting? Oh! ah! two simultaneous ejaculations. Two ditto actions. Walking in the damp grass our feet were again wet. We were content and happy.

Cooper was soon imitating Dad, while I played an accompaniment with two preludes, following Allen and Donnelly.

The grand finale was, bass fried to a delicious brown, eggs, bread and coffee.

Striking tents was done in a leisurely manner, to give the sun a chance at our wet dunnage. Packing damp things on a cruise is a feature that even the individual crank agrees is disagreeable.

Visitors in the shape of cattle invaded camp and sniffed about half timidly, half resentfully, at our usurping their domain.

Embarking, we glided down a little rift at Hankins, and just below caught several heavy drops. Running rifts, getting hung up on rocks and gravel bars, losing the channel and wading, was the order of the day. We summed up thirty-three rifts at the end of the day's trip, including the more noticeable Cochecton Falls.

At starting, we had a heavy wind at our backs, but the many twists and turns in our journey soon had us paddling dead against it.

Not only did this make heavy work, but it also caused faulty judgment in running rifts, impeding progress; in swifter water this state of affairs would have caused many accidents, possibly necessitating a stoppage altogether.

The reasons for exercising care in trimming canoes were now apparent. If too high in the bows, they would be blown about, and if the bows were down, the work would be harder, resulting also in wet craft.

Carter, whose study of shallow currents extends over a long period, exhibited a knowledge and skill that was almost infallible. He would size up an opening for what it was worth, immediately, from the set of the current, nature of rocks, amount and character of foam, etc., rejecting or accepting according to the indications.

During the whole trip he was only at fault four or five times, and then not seriously. The *Zerlina* came out without a scratch, and her captain with only an occasional wet foot.

The scenery on this day varied from that of yesterday, the mountains rising rock-bound on the right, while the hills to the left disappeared far in the interior, where they form a part of the Catskill mountains.

The fishing was not so good either, and the luck of our fishermen was not of the kind that furnished our morning's meal.

We reached Callicoon sometime after eleven o'clock, and calculated from the maps to reach Narrowsburg by night.

The toll-house at the bridge, the piles of lumber upon the sloping bank, and the low lying landscape, offered a fit scene for a photograph, and the camera was accordingly used to good effect.

Between the island and the town we were borne on a swift current, rounding to at the lower end, opposite Hollister creek. Landing, the cameras were brought to bear upon a perfect pastoral scene, which lay spread directly above us. It was a bit of hillside landscape that would have made a poem on canvas.

At the end of the island is a shallow ferry, and teams are constantly passing from the New York to the Pennsylvania shore.

Close to Pennsylvania we discovered entrance to a rocky rift. We steered through in safety, and found ourselves traversing a stretch of wild and mountainous country. At Cochecton, the uncleared, rock-bound cliffs, retreating, form a veritable wilderness. And yet, just beyond the barrier, one finds fertile valleys and fine farms, a romantic combination, surely.

Opposite the saw-mill we hauled over an obstruction in the shape of a log-boom. These booms are constructed and maintained illegally, and, at least, should be swung so as to allow the passage of small craft. Raftsmen cut their way through the booms unhesitatingly, whenever they encounter them. Just below, hidden from sight by a sharp bend, we could hear Cochecton Falls, the first really bad spot on the river.

Drifting to the upper ledge, we landed for an inspection. As we had anticipated, the rain of the night before had given us eight inches greater depth of water. This rise, however, was not sufficient to cover the rocks and ledges that were scattered in profuse in the fall. Neither could we discover any decided channel in the swiftly rushing torrent.

To run through safely would be a matter of the purest luck. With our loaded canoes it would be foolish to take the risk. Carter, who had run it on a "fresh," stated that the danger was great enough even then.

Enjoying a short rest, we entered our canoes, and passing over the first ledge, near the New York shore, landed on the huge table rock we found exposed. Enormous pot holes, worn by the action of gravel and water, were found in almost every rock in the ledge. We gathered the canoes at this point, and then guided them to a point half way down by means of bow and stern lines. Opposite the end of the fall was the worst place, and we had to "carry" over the rock to avoid it. Dropping the canoes into an extensive eddy, our task was completed.

And right here, I may state that the boys firmly resolved to fall over a precipice, should we meet one, rather than make another like "carry." It was the hardest work we did during the whole trip, and completely tired us for the rest of the day.

We were now traveling through what was at one time Indian stamping ground.

Cochecton is a corruption of the Lenâpé *Coquethagechton* meaning "White Eyes," the name of a celebrated Delaware chieftain.

Had it not been for the King's Commissioners, we would from Cochecton onward have been passing between New Jersey and Pennsylvania. The boundary line between New Jersey and New York, surveyed from the original grants, ran to Station Point, in latitude 41′ 40″. The present line, below Port Jervis, was run in 1769.

At noon, just above Cochecton, thinking to get some milk at a house that appeared behind a cluster of trees on a bluff on our right, Cooper and I went ashore and pushed through the underbrush until we came to a spring. From here a path led to the house. Clambering up, we reached the top only to meet with a scene of desolation.

The house was tenantless; doors were off hinges and windows broken. The out-buildings were dilapidated; floors broken, roofs dismantled and joists decayed.

> "Life and thought had gone away,
> Side by side,
> Leaving doors and windows wide,
> Careless tenants they."

Gathering some apples, and getting a delicious draught at the spring, we went back to the boats, and, for want of time to cook a meal, feasted on apples and bread.

Narrowsburg was now our objective point. Although we paddled rather briskly, the village was always "just around the next bend" with us. At least, this was the invariable response given by the natives when we inquired the distance to a given place. It became quite a side issue with our party.

At last we reached a point where, in rounding a bend, the river narrowed, and became so shallow that it looked as though we would have to carry across the gravel formation that jutted into the river from a hill on the right.

Going to the left of some large rocks, however, we found a channel, down which we scraped, to emerge directly into a narrow, rocky gorge. A little further, and we were floating on a currentless body of water, deep and black in the mountain's shadow—"Big Eddy," properly named. For the first time during our trip, we had to paddle to keep up headway. We also remarked the sudden coolness in the temperature.

Passing under the bridge, which is built out of the reach of the highest freshet, we pushed through the foam-flecked water past numerous fishing parties.

At last, rounding an abrupt bend, we saw ahead a low lying island, to which we paddled in search of a campsite.

The island affording no inducement for making a camp, we turned toward the grassy slopes on the Pennsylvania shore, and, close to the dividing line between Wayne and Pike counties, pitched our camp. We were on the frontier. In the interior, and not so very far either, trout, bass, pickerel, deer, bear and grouse are in waiting for the hardy woodsman.

It was now six o'clock, and the sun had left us for the day. As we were in need of provisions, we thought it expeditious to get supper in the village, and to make purchases.

Donnelly, Allen and I unpacked and made ready for the night, while Carter and Cooper went over the bridge in search of a hotel.

An hour later we, as the second detachment, repaired to the "Arlington," whither Carter had directed us, as host Gutheil was expecting a second invasion. Passing through the office and upstairs to the spacious dining rooms, we found spread before us a meal in keeping with the surroundings.

As if to enliven our tired wit, we found our guardian angel in the person of Fraulein Gutheil, business-like and efficient. Her laughing eyes, pearly teeth and vivacious manners were irresistible.

Our grace before meat, each to the other, was in the language of Shakespeare, "God comfort thy capacity." The meal admitted of no disparaging comments. It was solid worth and squared by rule. We left, feeling at peace with the country and the house of Arlington. Besides, we carried away with us two substantial loaves of home-made bread, bestowed upon us as a special favor by Frau Gutheil. Of course, the intercession in our behalf of her worthy daughter had nothing to do with the case.

Taking a short walk, we saw the sights and made some purchases, and then went back to camp by the mountain path bathed in a flood of moonlight. To right and left, before and behind, the steep hills formed a mountain pocket, containing a vast body of water, the outlet from which, in our position, we could not discover. On reaching camp, we found the boys had made a cheerful fire, the night being cool and promising frost. From a native, who dropped in on us, we learned that the pool in front of our camp was sixty-five feet deep and absolutely without current. This is owing to the curious formation of the valley above and below, and the great depth at the bend. During high water there are two eddies so great that rafts running the river have not sufficient momentum to carry them through the dead water. Consequently, the rafts have to be towed until they reach the downward current.

For this purpose ropes are carried to the island, opposite the bend, down which the raftsmen walk with their tow. This is the only spot, from Arkville to Trenton, where this hauling has to be done.

During the rafting season, the vicinity of the eddy is one of great activity, and not a little confusion.

Turning in after a day of labor, we took a last look at the orb of night hanging over the motionless waters of "Big Eddy." It was a picture not likely to be forgotten—too enchanting to be easily dismissed from the memory.

CHAPTER 5.

A Delaware Highlands Morning.
A Day of Comparisons.
Wild Scenery.
River Currents.
Masthope Rift.
Blooming Grove Park.
Lackawaxen.
Shooting the Dam.
Shohola.
A Bad Rift.
Camp-Fire Reveries.

These, as they change, Almighty Father, these
Are but the varied God.—*Thomson*.

"UP YE sluggards, and see the day break!" It was
Carter calling, and, heeding him, I turned out.

The morning was crisp and frosty. Allen was
already out, and Cooper, sleepy and barefoot, soon followed suit. And Donnelly? Deep down in a board-thick
army blanket that canoeist lay fast asleep. The cows might
have been in the corn, the sun melting icicles, or the Boo-
jum Snark invading the Gurzigazoon, but Donnelly was
dreaming.

The night had been cool. Wood was scarce in our
locality, and the camp-fire embers were long since cold.
So toward morning I buried my head, ears and nose in
the warmth of a thick-knitted Tam o' Shanter.

While we were busying ourselves with early morning
camp duties the sun burst in radiance over the eastern
hills, flooding the camp with warmth, and the surrounding
valley with brightness.

The morning was a typical Delaware Highlands morning, and we were in high feather, glad that we were alive.

The evolutions of the trio, Carter, Donnelly and Allen,
in getting arrayed for breakfast at the hotel, commanded
attention. All on account of the pretty waitress. Cooper and
I at our ease, *en deshabille*, cooked a hearty camp breakfast
of potatoes, eggs, onions and coffee, with delicious home-
made bread and Orange county butter.

After our meal Cooper, taking the *Nahiwi*, paddled above the camp for an exposure, getting the bridge and Big Eddy, looking down stream.

The absent ones returned to the fold about eight o'clock. An hour later we were packed and afloat, taking with us pleasant recollections of a pleasant camping spot.

Anticipating the narrative, we made camp at 5:30 o'clock in the afternoon, just before reaching Parker's Glen, having made eighteen miles from the time of leaving Narrowsburg.

For weather and rapids, it was a day to be remembered. Keeping account of the latter, we ran thirty-one, big and little, without a single mishap.

The weather and scenery also vied with each other, and each in its different way contributed to our enjoyment. For comparative study we had sunshine and peaceful stretches of farmland; we had sun-showers and rolling, pine-covered hills; we had thunderstorms and clouds, and rugged, rocky mountain cliffs.

In the river we encountered quiet currents and foam-lashed, thunder-booming torrents. For extremes, we had Big Eddy and Lackawaxen Dam; for intermediates Tusten Rift and Shohola Falls.

But to retrace our steps. Below Narrowsburg we entered a long, shallow rift with a crooked channel, which finally flowed close under the foot of the mountain. We got through safely, and during the day ran rifts so continually that we were on a constant strain taking care of our canoes.

An explanation is in place right here. A keel canoe is the proper one for river cruising. The keel should be broad, flat and of tough wood, for the river bed is composed of gravel and boulders, on which, in shallow water, the canoe is constantly pounding.

As we drifted onward, the wildness and grandeur of our surroundings became more marked.

High and ever-changing hills and mountain ranges loomed about us on every hand. Far away in the distance faint outlines of southern hills were traceable.

From Narrowsburg to Lackawaxen there still remains a famous bass fishing section. Those caught by our fishermen were numerous and large. And one and all discussed the feasability of a fishing camp at some future time. A two or three weeks' stay would ensure plenty of sport at this season of the year with both rod and gun.

On either hand extend forests of pine, beech, hemlock and chestnut. The lumber interests are valuable, and with the farm lands in the fertile valleys, which the mountain streams make numerous, and the slate and stone quarries, form the industries of the settlers.

Where the Erie railroad crosses the river, at Tusten, or Pine Grove, we met with a heavy rift somewhat dangerous on account of its formation. We had marked, from the car window, on our ride to Hancock, a ledge of rocks from shore to shore, just under the bridge. It seemed shallow, and we were dubious about getting through. Actually in the rift, we found more water than appeared from a distance. In the waters below the rift as we shot through, Donnelly hooked a fine pickerel.

After getting a photograph, we paddled down to a small rift, in which Cooper provokingly broke his paddle. How it happened, he was at a loss to know; it might have been injured in the heavier water at Tusten. Fortunately, it was a long split, which was spliced and wrapped as we floated downstream.

We floated through two or three little rushes, during the paddle-mending incident, but finally had to complete it hastily, as we were bearing down on a heavier rift.

In traveling the Delaware, it behooves the *voyageur* to be careful and wide-awake at all times. He never knows the kind of water ahead. A different stage of water, either lower or higher, completely changes the formation, and even the location of the smaller rifts and falls. Their channels and dangerous ledges also may be changed from a few feet to the entire width of the river. To drift downstream broadside, or with unjointed blades, is the height of recklessness.

Late in the morning we reached Masthope. This little place (noted for its stone quarries) can hardly be passed by the traveler on the Delaware without remarking its peculiar surroundings.

On the right, just before entering swift water, Masthope creek tumbles into the larger body; below, on the bank, stands a grove of cedars, each trunk as stiff and orderly as if belonging to a detachment of pickets. On the opposite bank rises rocky pine-clad cliffs. Ahead is Big Cedar Rift, a mile and a half long. Entering this the bend places the town at your back. As we began to feel the force of the current the sky clouded and a few drops of rain fell.

We found the rift a bad one, the fall being great and the volume of water heavy. Add to this length of the rift its uncertain channel and rocky ledges, and it would be bad enough on a clear day.

On this day the combination was anything but pleasant. Before rounding the last bend, from which the foot was visible, we several times rested in the friendly eddies that form on the lower side of exposed rocks.

Once through, we had better water, and during a paddle of three miles were skirting the game and fish preserves of the Blooming Grove Park association, and the Pike County Hunting and Fishing club.

These associations own about twenty-eight thousand acres of the choicest waters and estates in this region, embracing some magnificent scenery.

Overlooking the river and commanding a grand view of the fertile valley, the associations have large and finely-appointed club houses.

Opposite the boat landing, a rugged, pine-clad hill of gray rock rises from the depths. A curious feature is a growth of gnarled pines, whose tenacious roots find substance in the frost-split interstices.

A number of photographs were taken of the exquisite bits of landscape that rapidly came into view.

Around the bend we scraped over a bar that extends to the slack water above Lackawaxen. The sudden entrance to the beautiful country about this station is sure to occasion outbursts of admiration. In our case the view was enhanced by the breaking away of rain clouds, and the appearance of the sun to lighten up the peaceful scene. The face of the country partakes of the placidity of the huge volume of water, which is held back by an enormous dam, just below the mouth of the creek.

Lackawaxen is a great summer resort, and the country round-about contains many points of interest.

While drifting down, we had lunch, and at one o'clock lined up along the right-hand bank below the large white hotel, the Delaware House, and above the sluiceway through the dam.

The Delaware and Hudson canal, beginning at Honesdale, Pennsylvania, follows the windings of the Lackawaxen river to its mouth, crosses the Delaware river, and continues in New York state, by way of Delaware river, to Port Jervis, and then along the foot of the sinuous Shawangunk mountain range to Eddyville on Rondout creek.

The dam built across the river at this point is owned by the Delaware and Hudson canal company. It is sixteen feet high, constructed in the most approved scientific manner, to secure strength.

During the rafting season, the opening for rafts is in the center.

Many stories of hair-breadth escapes in running this shute are told by all old raftsmen, and the spot is indeed a dangerous one, so much so that the company, which is a private corporation, is held responsible by the two states for all accidents to rafts incurred while going through. During the season a pilot is furnished, whose duty it is to take charge until each raft is safely through. Notwithstanding this many accidents occur, as the least faulty judgment in the mad rush will break up the mass of timber in a twinkling.

The drop during a "fresh" is very great, causing a long raft to make such a bend that the bow-man cannot see the steersman until the raft straightens out. The plunge is so severe that the forward end goes completely under, drenching all hands.

We found the sluiceway on the right shore nearly closed by a temporary wing to facilitate repairs.

The opening was only twelve feet wide, through which the water shot at surprising speed. We judged the rate to be about a mile per minute. The solid volume of water held itself compact for a distance of fifteen feet, with a drop of eight feet, taken in two inclines.

This huge wave then bore straight downward, by its force sending upward two boat lengths away a foamer sixteen feet in height. Swift rough water followed, between the bank and the first wing, in which racks of slabs are anchored to protect the river bed. A swift shoot under the bridge, ending in a wave-filled tail-race, completes the description.

After some reconnoitering, and testing the channel with heavy oak slabs, which were whisked into the foam in a twinkling, we decided upon our course.

Carter took it first, in the *Zerlina*, Allen catching a photograph as he was in the act of breaking through the crest.

Cooper followed the leader, first removing camera and blankets. He went over safely, although his broken blade was twisted in two, leaving him to finish with half a paddle.

Donnelly and the *Nahiwi* followed suit in safety.

It was a great feat, and one of which to be proud. The sight, too, was a pretty one, and full of life. Away above the edge the blades of the paddles flashed in the sunlight. Instantly the canoe appears, the occupant's face worthy of study as he braces himself for the shock and its results— good or bad. Quick as a camera shutter drops, the boat and her crew were pitched from the wave into the crest, held aloft for an instant, revealing the boat's bottom from stem to stern; then breaking through, dropped into the swift water.

It is over the minute you reach the edge, but you are in the grasp of a demon, and you hold your breath hard. A slip, an upset, and the cribs, ballast and spike-strewn logs below may determine the commencement of a cruise into the great unknown, on a pink cloud, in the ethereal blue.

Rounding the cribs below, the race is run and a deep eddy welcomes the bonny craft.

The *Werowance* being only twelve feet by twenty-six inches beam, Allen decided not to take the risk, and so slid over the fishway.

Below the bridge we stopped and effected needed repairs. Cooper recovered the lost blade and renewed his paddle by cutting back and resetting the ferrule. The only inconvenience was due to its shortening. There were more rifts as we continued, but after our recent shaking up they appeared tame. The river became narrow, flowing through a veritable gate in the mountain. The country was wild, rolling from range to range as far as eye could see.

At 3:45 o'clock in the afternoon we ran ashore at Shohola, under clouds and in rain.

We were all in good spirits and hungry. Facing the river was the Spring House. Provisions with us were low. Proceeding on our journey meant a damp camp and a damp bit of cookery. Bunching canoes, we had a call of the roll. Too tempting. All lazy. Result—we stopped for dinner.

At the house we were very nicely served. It should be a fine summer retreat, for, besides its nearness to all points of interest, it commands a fine view of the river and valley.

The vicinity of Shohola is noted for its mountain scenery. The Glen, containing wonderful cascades, waterfalls and rocky caverns, is but a short distance from the town. Hardby are several trout streams, having their sources in the Sullivan Highlands.

Although it was rather early, we fared well, and three quarters of an hour after landing, five cruisers were replete with five different portions of potatoes, eggs, beef, tomatoes, pudding, pie and coffee.

It continued raining, but it was all in the experience. Clad in oilskins, we proceeded until we got hung up in what someone remarked was "mid-chick" rift. It merged into the well-known Shohola falls so suddenly that its growth from a chicken to a full-sized fighting-cock permitted no intermediate stage.

As Carter was leading through he bumped broadside against a submerged rock. His agility in getting out saved an upset. Each canoeist picked a channel as best he could. The place was narrow and thickly strewn with rocks, the current swift, and the turns frequent and sharp. We struck repeatedly. At the last rush, Donnelly and Cooper were both carried down on the *Nahiwi*, and all labored through together, waves from three to four feet high, and choppy from conflicting currents, swashed us from stem to stern, but the little *Werowance* behaved herself nobly.

Still there were more to follow. We took them and the attendant wetting until half-past five, when we came across a campsite at the base of the canal bank.

It was a level, grassy place, in rather low ground, but we could drive tent pegs, without the difficulty heretofore encountered. Hauling out, we soon had the tents erected in a half circle with a camp-fire place in the opening.

It was showering fitfully, but we had hopes of its discontinuance. Foraging parties soon had a pile of hard-wood ties and planks, and a lasting fire was scientifically laid. When the blaze became a glowing, we drew our chairs within the warmth, enjoying it immensely, and drying wet garments. Cooper and I took a river bath in the swift flow at the foot of camp, and then added a hot shampoo.

The Quartermaster got up an impromptu lunch for the party, finding the delicacies from his ample store. He explained that he must do something to lighten his load for the morrow's paddle.

The country through which we traveled this day was entirely different in point of scenery from that of previous days. We skirted pine-clad hills and rocky cliffs, and pleasant sloping bluffs. All about our camp were wild hills. Opposite, on a heavy grade, ran the tracks of the Erie railroad. We could hear the engines puff and the wheels slip, and see the reflected glow from the fires as the furnace doors were thrown back.

From Lackawaxen to Port Jervis we were to be accompanied by the Delaware and Hudson canal, with the ever-attendant noise of horns and shoutings, together with the choice vocabulary of captains and mule drivers.

We greatly enjoyed the camp-fire. After the trying experiences of the day the rest and cheerfulness was welcomed by all.

I do not doubt but that every cruiser and camper counts as lost the night passed without the blaze of the camp fire, whether the blaze be great or small. To the party grouped about, it lends a fluency to conversation as it leaps and crackles and glows red in the darkness. To the solitary cruiser it is a companion. Its warmth and light prevents feelings of loneliness and longing. To the dreamer and the poet it lends visions and language. As its flames break forth, or its thin curls of smoke twine aloft, it becomes a most trustworthy confidant. What reflections it reveals! what faces! what forms it conjures up! It smokes and smoulders at starting, as you sit before it delving into the dim past.

It brightens and warms as your impulses deal with thoughts of the present. It is a sympathetic friend. You would see into the future? Your mind, unsatisfied, gives up the task, and the fire in sympathy settles and sighs, tries to resume the thread, flickers and leaves you with your vain quest in confusing darkness. It is out and you retire. Secrets uttered aloud it remembereth not. Joys and sorrows it never repeats.

CHAPTER 6.

A Dream.
Poetry.
A Hot Day.
Parker's Glen.
Lost Channel Rift.
Mongaup Falls.
Heavy Water.
Baptising a Canoe.
Butler's Falls.
Above Port Jervis.
Tri-State Monument.
Marking a Boundary Line.
Geological Formations.
Glimmer Glass.
A Little French.

On sunny slope and beechen swell,
The shadowed light of evening fell;
And, where the maple's leaf was brown,
With soft and silent lapse came down,
The glory, that the wood receives,
At sunset, in its golden leaves.—*Longfellow.*

AN ODD dream disturbed my sleep toward morn-ing. Connecting the threads, it worked itself out about as follows:

I dreamed that after the night's camp we had packed canoes and journeyed onward. Having gone but a short distance, we ran down to a small fishery in a wide arm of the river. As we reached the gravel, the following was noted at a glance:

Close to the water's edge lay a tangled net, two wheel-barrows, and two piles of freshly-caught fish. Slightly to the left we saw two burly fishermen berating each other with tongues and fists.

As we drifted down, I imagined I heard Cooper sing out, "A nice way to start the morning, pardners! What's the row?"

Both contestants, seemingly anxious for arbitration, ran toward us.

Said one, "D'ye see surs, Bill he wouldn't divide the catch fair, and kept all the big wans."

"I didn't neither," chimed in Bill, "Besides, don't I own the net?"

"A heap you'd a got with yer net if I hadn't a helped ye."

"Now, listen to 'm," sarcastically ejaculated number two. "Ain't I right, gentlemen?"

"I leave it you, if he has divided fair."

All the above was said thick and fast, and we got more information from the surroundings than from the jargon.

"Court will come to order," said Donnelly in mock severity. "Go ahead with the summing up, Dad."

We had drifted into shore with Carter in the center, Donnelly and Allen on his left, and Cooper and I up stream.

Judge, jury, court constables, stenographers and notary, with two prosecutors, who were likewise defendants and plaintiffs from and of themselves, we proceeded with the celebrated case.

Each of the principals repeated his story with glowing looks, making a few additions to his first outburst. When each had finished, Judge Carter, for the time being, recounted as follows:

"Gentlemen, you are both right" (here the two worthies looked quizzical), "and you are both wrong" (here they looked indignant). "Taking the case at its present status, one charges dishonesty in the division of the haul. The other claims the right to the larger share from ownership of the net. To this latter claim the matter of assistance is used as an offset.

"Gentlemen, these points in the case I do not consider warrant attention from the force of circumstances. We will overlook them, and pursue another course in the solution of the controversy. From appearances, I take it that you are neighbors, depending upon one another for many small favors in daily life. You have lived peaceably for a long time. Why should you not continue to do so? You both live and breathe the free air which a great and good God, having required you to need, supplies in abundance. You have to fight no one for it. It is natural for you. You breathe it, and, I have no doubt, forget to thank Him to whom you are indebted.

"Together, you, in friendliness, came here for fish, both for food and to convert them by sale into money, with which to purchase articles needful to life. These fish are not yours; you did not place them here; you have asked permission of no one; you just come and appropriate that which enables you to get greater personal comforts. And the result: having netted a goodly supply, you forget everything—friendship, charity, equity—for selfishness."

The most righteous judge turned toward the jury as if to ask a verdict, but of this there was no need. The verdict, in accordance with truth and justice, had been anticipated, even by the untutored fishermen.

From anger the mind of each man had turned to doubt, and from doubt to enlightenment and remorse. Before Carter had ceased speaking I saw them making up in characteristic style, the net owner throwing all the big fish over to the smaller pile, amid protestations from his companion, both muttering rude apologies. They then loaded the barrows, each assisting the other as gleefully as two school boys on a frolic, each claiming also the right to bear the additional burden of the net.

This settled, they generously helped each other up the steep incline to the plateau above.

My feet had pushed through the blankets and against the cold, damp tent, sending a "chilly flow" along my vertebra. This may account for the dream.

I lost no time in folding them in the warmth of the blankets, and lay musing over the foregoing deductions.

Outside, the "foggy, foggy dew" was slowly drifting up stream, blown by a faint breeze.

Tinkle, tinkle, tinkle. Down the tow-path, close by, comes an early canal boat with its team of mules, its captain and the muleteer. We are objects of curiosity to all the animated creatures until a bend hides us from view.

We got breakfast by the embers of last night's campfire, using chairs for tables and rocks for seats.

Cleaning up and loading canoes occupied our time, according to rule, Carter meanwhile quoting snatches of poetry. At this we wondered, as Carter's opinion, candidly expressed, is "I have no use for a man who murders good prose in order to express himself by bad versification."

We were afloat as the sun broke through the mist. Hot? Don't mention it.

At Parker's Glen we stopped to get a photograph of a natural waterspout that shot some fifty feet in air. It made its exit from the bowels of the earth through a fissure in the rock. The spout was on a bluff above the river, with a dark-green mountain side for a background. The gentle morning breeze dissipated the falling stream into misty arches, the sun completing the spectacle by transforming the whole into miniature rainbows.

Nestling in the pines, among the hills, and commanding a wide sweep of glen and river, we noticed a large hotel and several dwellings.

Opposite the village we ran an unusual kind of rift. There was no definite channel, and we were compelled to dodge in and out among sharp rocks as best we could until through. From shore to shore the current swept resistless, apparently of uniform depth, broken and riffled from countless causes. We dubbed it Lost Channel Rift.

During the day's journey the channel led us under

immense rocky cliffs, rising first from one side of the river and then from the other, the Pennsylvania side, however, being the more precipitous. Scraggly pine trees covered the hillside.

The rifts we found very shallow, and with sharp descents, winding up at the foot in chop cross-currents with turbulent waves. Thus we traveled, encountering in some places two or three descents in quick succession. The bends, too, were sharper and more frequent.

At ten o'clock we were skirting the canal wall at Pond Eddy. Just beyond the village, Allen obtained a fine picture, the rock-bound ending of a rolling mountain range.

Two miles further down the river, and we heard a heavy booming that caused us to train our eyesight ahead.

In the distance we could see a narrow, rocky channel, down which the foam-lashed volume poured with such force that waves six feet in height were formed. And this is Mongaup Falls. It is not long, but it is very juicy, what there is of it, and, as the boy said, there is lots of it, such as it is. The river and town of the same name lay on the right.

Our experience at this point proved a rough teacher. We had grown so familiar with "rifts" that we welcomed them merely as helps in our journey. We had as yet no thought of recurring to our lap covers, not having met with currents sufficiently heavy to swamp us.

However, we were destined to grow familiar with sterner things. The heavier body of water obliterated the rifts, and falls were now to engage our combined tact and strength—Mongaup, Butler's, Sawyer's, Buttermilk, Bull's Island, Wells', Scudder's and Trenton. At Mongaup we strung out, the *Zerlina* in the lead, then *Werowance*, *Nyleptha*, *Nahiwi*, and the Quartermaster, the latter trolling. Incidentally, he hooked a fine bass in the deep water, carrying it through only to lose it when hauling it in at the foot of the fall.

As the *Nahiwi* shot in, she went down over the crest, and then upward on a wave that made me lean back with bated breath. I threw my weight aft as far as possible to keep her nose out of the wave crests, but it was a failure. The canoe shipped enough of the second one to make her pitch log-like into the next. In the third she was awash completely. I kept her straight until out of the worst of it, and then made for a rocky point on the right.

We reached shallow water just in time for the canoe to gracefully settle on the bottom with all on board.

It was over in a short space of time, and accomplished so neatly that we laughed over the incident merely at its recollection. We all caught it, and had to bail out canoes for the first time since starting.

Here I must digress to state that in these falls Donnelly's handsome Bowdish canoe was christened, in a baptism of violence, *Eulalia Mongaup*. She started out a new boat, and nameless. We had partially known her as *Eulalia*, in honor of the parlor car in which we traveled to Hancock. The latter addition, later in the trip, gave such a classical Indian-German finish that it was irresistable. And as for the sex, if in this respect there is any doubt, the *Lily Gaup* settles it forever.

Almost in the shadow of Hawk's Nest Peak, at the head of the usual bend, we ran Butler's Falls, deep and rough. This is a bad place, owing to the unnatural confinement of the waters by the high canal wall. The worst waves can be avoided by veering to the right after taking the entering pitch, but one is liable to catch the side waves over the gunwale. The plunge at the foot cannot be avoided. The easiest way, and that giving the sport desired, is to ride the heavy waves in the channel.

A short distance up the side of the cliff winds the road, and a couple of farmers stopped to watch our tiny barks ride the crests, uttering exclamations in open-mouthed astonishment. From the height our canoes must, indeed, have seemed small.

Out of this, and running a short, smooth reach, we met with Sawyer's, or Sawmill Falls. We worked our passage through its long and heavy right-hand channel, until we labored under the railroad bridge.

In a cove at the base of Prospect Hill range, out of the winds and waves, we gathered to rest. Here, where the waves gently lapped the rocks, we found a native fisherman snugly ensconced, luring the gamey bass from the swift channel beyond.

While resting and taking appreciative views of the landscape spread before us, we noticed, high above on the cliffside, covered with moss, ferns and pines, a "flying buttress." The whole was so catchy that a couple of photographs were taken.

As we pushed out into the stream we were mere specks in the turbulent, narrow channel at the foot of the rocky range. The surroundings can easily be likened to one of the Colorados noted cañons. At the end of the gorge we floated to the crest of a smooth, shallow incline, down which we glided, bringing up under the bridge at Port Jervis. We were glad to get out of the hot sun, and counted the completion of seventy-five miles of what was turning out to be a most delightful vacation cruise.

Hauling out canoes, we went up into town for needed supplies; to the shoe-dealer's (wading is hard on the foot gear); to the post-office, for word from the dear ones at home, and praying to receive no urgent recall to business duties; to the express-office, for Allen's extra blades, and to ship home the dry plates containing precious materialized memories.

"Port," as the town is familiarly called in the region adjacent, has a population of fifteen thousand souls, and is the central point from which can be reached numerous summer resorts. Stage lines to mountain retreats in the three states do a thriving business in summer. The Monticello railroad branch also has considerable traffic. In view of its industries—railroad shops, manufactories, etc.—the town holds rank with other larger cities in New York state. As for the scenery, the view from the railroad, just before entering the town, is one long to be remembered, so peaceful and romantic withal.

High Point, to the eastward, and not far from Milford, Pennsylvania, in a direct line, is a noted resort among the Shawangunk mountains (or shaw'n-gum in the vernacular). Here the valley begins to widen; low sloping swells, brown in the autumn, could be clearly traced. Valleys and pleasant nooks are synonymous with the name of Neversink. Minisink Plain is just beyond the range, and this in itself brings recollections of times agone.

The day was not far advanced, and we decided to make Milford, seven miles below, in time to camp. Milford is reached from Port Jervis by the "White Hat" stage line, over a hard mountain road.

But we are not going that way. Just below the bridge, and the town, the river is cut up by gravel bars. Consequently, a rocky and shoal rift is met, which continues to the mouth of the Neversink river.

At this junction the southwest boundary of southern New York state comes to an angle, and turns due west (475 feet). West of this point, in the center of the Delaware river, lies imbedded the corner-stone between New York, New Jersey and Pennsylvania. Across the mouth of the Neversink, the northwest boundary of New Jersey comes to a point. Looking westward, the center of Pike county, the beginning of the north boundary of Pennsylvania pokes its nose into a point.

Here in New York state the Delaware and Hudson canal winds off on its way to Rondout and the Hudson, while the Erie railroad curves up on its way to Buffalo. The extreme southern angle of the state has its vertex in the local cemetery.

Running our canoes into a bank of sand, we landed on the point in New York, to view like other curiosity seekers the Tri-State Rock, situated on the very termination of a rocky formation, and also to see the boundary monument, 72 ¼ feet above it, on a rising knoll.

Fifteen years ago the stone that was originally erected to mark the outlines was carried away by a freshet. After that a brass rod, having the lines sunken on the flat surface, was mortised into the rock. In 1882 the present mark was affixed to the rock by the joint commission of the three states, appointed by the governors to perpetuate the record.

To the present generation the boundary line carries a deep significance, being as it is the straight line between savagery and civilization. As we viewed the fettered surroundings, our minds reverted to the pristine beauty of the place when the red men hunted, fished and roamed at will, beaching their canoes at the rocky point, even as we had, to form their nightly camp.

The monument on the knoll is of polished granite, and has carved upon its face the following:

NEW YORK
BOUNDARY MONUMENT.
1882

HENRY R. PIERSON.
ELIAS W. LEAVENWORTH.
CHAUNCEY M. DEPEW.
COMMISSIONERS.

H. W. CLARKE
SURVEYOR.

THE CORNER-STONE BETWEEN NEW YORK
& PENNSYLVANIA IS IN THE CENTRE OF THE
DELAWARE RIVER, 475 FEET DUE WEST OF THE
TRI-STATE ROCK.
Facing westerly.

NEW JERSEY
BOUNDARY MONUMENT.
1882

ABRAHAM BROWNING.
THOMAS N. McCARTER.
GEORGE H. COOKE.
COMMISSIONERS.

E. A. BOWSER
SURVEYOR.

SOUTH, 84 DEGREES W. 72 ¼ FT. FROM THIS IS

THE TRI-STATE ROCK WHICH IS THE NORTH-
WEST END OF THE NEW YORK & NEW JERSEY
BOUNDARY AND THE NORTH END OF THE NEW
JERSEY & PENNSYLVANIA BOUNDARY.
Facing easterly.

The boundary line between New York and New Jersey was long a subject of dispute. In 1774, the assemblies of the colonies of New York and New Jersey (Nova Caesarea) appointed commissions for the purpose of confirming titles and possessions. The commissioners for New York were William Wickham and Samuel Gale; for New Jersey, John Stevens and Walter Rutherford.

Under the joint commission the present boundary line was run by two surveyors, representing the two states. Their certificate corrected the old survey "by staking that from the station rock, marked on the west side of Hudson river, in the latitude of forty-one degrees, to the fork or branch formed by the junction of the stream, or waters called the Machockemack, with the river called Delaware, or Fishkill."

The trees along the line of the new survey were marked with a blaze and five notches under the same. At a distance of one mile apart, forty-eight stone monuments were set, each containing on its north side the words "New York," and on the south side the words "New Jersey." The total distance was forty-eight miles and thirty-eight chains.

From the boundary monument the view is grand. To us it was like bursting from the mountains and beholding the pleasant paths of peace. Close at hand, forming a charming picture, the Neversink merged with the Delaware. It was a diorama of one of nature's most lavish moods.

Ahead the country spread out into far-reaching hills and fertile plains, forming, in the sunlight, as Cooper remarked, a perfect Scotch landscape.

> "Never did sun more beautifuly steep
> In his first splendor, valley, rock, or hill;
> Ne'er saw I, never felt, a calm so deep!
> The river glideth at its own sweet will."

We traveled in this section during the best part of a pleasant afternoon, skirting the base of the Highland Range foot hills. As we proceeded, we found that we had left the mountains. We picked up the lost thread below Milford, when we met with the continuation of the Appalachian chain, the Blue mountains, about Water Gap. Thence the valley widens for two or three miles, the ranges disappear and are gradually left behind. We passed several islands and plenty of pretty scenes, which were lost and found at the rounding of each successive bend.

After leaving Port Jervis, we noticed for a long distance a very remarkable geological formation, that lay exposed above water-mark. It had the appearance of having been at one time subjected to melting heat, and then agitated so that it had taken on jagged and wavelike forms (or outlines) before cooling.

We were still traveling in the limestone section belonging to the upper Helderberg epoch, but this was the first appearance of Cherty limestone beds with the hornstone exposed.

The action of the water had worn away the limestone, leaving the peculiar conglomerate. Inside the knodules we found a liquid pitch, supposedly caused by the sun's heat.

At five o'clock we drifted into the wide arm of the river

at Milford, finding the exact counterpart of Fenimore Cooper's word picture of the Glimmerglass. The minutest shadow was reflected with exactness, and not a ripple broke the surface to the next bend. We pitched our tents near the boat landing, at the base of the cliff, on which is had one of the finest drives in the section.

Donnelly was bound we should stop over night, promising a fine meal at the Hotel Fauchere. We were in prime condition to discuss a hearty meal, whether served in Parisian or American style. The claim of this meal to the former style was based upon the service of hot plates, warm milk and elegant and *ennuied* dinners.***

The evening was cool, and the moonlight revealed from our camp and from the bluff a grand view of fertile plain and winding river, bathed in the soft light.

The influence of the surroundings manifested itself in many ways. Donnelly, who affects tragedy, regaled us with some heavy Shakespearean passages. Carter and Cooper indulged in reminiscences of travel through European countries, and Allen botanized, and theorized on instantaneous photography.

And the scribe? Well, the scribe has a bad habit of "thinking and smoking tobacco." That he enjoyed the passage of the evening is evident from his assertion that "the night's camp at Milford was remembered as one of the most pleasant of the trip."

*** NOTE.—If the cruiser expects to follow this kind of living, extras must include a freight canoe as a tender to contain full-dress suits, white flannel outing suits, sashes, patent leathers, silk underwear, freckle and tan lotions, almond meal, brilliantine and a barber.

J. WALLACE HOFF

CHAPTER 7.

Milford, Pennsylvania.
Sawkill Falls.
"Coming Events Cast Their Shadows Before."
Eel Racks.
In the Delaware Valley.
We Astonish a Native.
Rest and Revery.
The First Accident.
Walpack Bend.
A Moonlight Scene.
Early History.

Lo! dusky masses steal in dubious sight
Along the leaguered wall, and bristling bank
Of the armed river.—*Byron.*

T**HE** dampness of Mongaup Falls proved penetrating. I turned out at 6 o'clock, after a night in wet blankets. Trees, bushes, and the very ground dripped with the cold, clinging fog. Climbing up the mountain side, I had a discouraging search for firewood. Once back in camp, the boys were soon routed out and a fire started. Cooper and I cooked a delicious breakfast of chops, eggs and coffee, and the others—the dudes—went up into town for a hotel breakfast.

Milford is the county seat of Pike county, and has a population of about 800. It is most charmingly situated on a broad, rolling formation, some two hundred feet above the river, yet at the base of higher mountains further inland.

We had arranged for the local stage to stop for us at seven o'clock, as we wished to view the Sawkill Falls, about a mile inland, reached by a mountain road.

Gathering our party, we drove up into the town over hard roads winding through rows of stately maples. We turned into the road leading through the princely domains of Banker Pinchot, who owns, with other lands, the Glen containing Sawkill Falls. The grounds are most generously thrown open to tourists and residents.

The road and the path to the Falls are marvels of beauty, winding as they do in full view of "Gray Castle," with its commodious lawns, and under fairy bowers of feathery spruce and pine.

Reaching the forest we tied the team, and with our guide continued afoot, disappearing into the romantic labyrinth.

Ahead we heard sharp sounds, as of water falling from a great height. A sudden turn in the path brought us face to face with a pretty bit of rugged nature in solitude. And the noise—

> 'Tis only the torrent, tumbling o'er,
> In the midst of those glassy walls,
> Gushing and plunging, and beating the floor
> Of the rocky basin in which it falls.

At our feet was a deep and wide chasm lined with jagged black rocks, covered with moisture. Opposite us, and higher still, the mountain stream, like a huge bridal veil, tumbled over a rocky wall to be churned to foam in its journey over the cliff's side.

Into a deep rock-basin it fell, continuing to the river through a gorge, down which it plunged, a narrow green stream, deep and rock confined.

We clambered over the slippery, moss-covered boulders to the pool, and inspected the "Devil's Kitchen" and the "Winding Cañon."

The sun glistened upon the scene, affording just the light for taking photographs.

Beyond, the Knob and Pike's Peak loomed up boldly, but our time was limited, and next to Conashaugh Spring we had seen the prettiest spot at all hazards.

On our way back to camp, we learned that our guide had been a raftsman during the prime of lumbering in the regions round about, and from him we became posted on that portion of the river down which we were yet to travel.

On our arrival at Port Jervis, we had been questioned as to our purpose to run Foul Rift, about a mile below Belvidere, and were warned not to attempt it.

Our guide also brought up the subject, and cautioned us to be careful, if we decided to risk it, and to keep the Pennsylvania channel if we could.

As an exciting incident of his own rafting experience, he told us how, at one time, his raft being overtaken by another, just before entering Wells' Falls, at Lambertville, the two were lashed together, side by side, and piloted through safely.

The width of the channel at Wells' is about ninety-five feet, and that of two rafts ninety feet. To accomplish the undertaking required a steady nerve, coupled with plenty of daring, as one familiar with the place will acknowledge.

Stopping in town for provisions and tent pegs (which latter we vowed should be iron when we essayed another cruise), we went back to camp and struck tents, not getting under way, however, until after ten o'clock. Our fortunate cruise, thus far, seemed to strike the natives as remarkable.

A boatman at Milford put the usual question, and we replied that we had run all the rapids but those at Cochecton.

In an undertone, we heard him doubt it to a companion, saying that he was acquainted with the river from having made the trip on a raft, and he knew it could not be done in a canoe.

We paddled down the pond-like opening until we reached the point below the landing. Here the current shallowed, and babbled over a gravel bar. The channel ran directly down hill to the right, and then wound along the base of a bluff.

The foot of the rift proved to be an eel-rack, and we did not notice it until we were nearing the apex of trap, when it was too late to back out of the rush. Cooper and I were ahead, and we passed through safely, finding the opening between two large rocks. Beyond was deep water again. Allen fouled Carter and swamped, jumping out just before going over the side wall. It required some exertion in the swift running current to get the water-logged craft ashore. We had to work waist deep in water, and gradually trend up stream. Reaching shore, the canoe was emptied and then repacked.

The accident was unfortunate, as it occasioned the loss of several exposed plates, and the spoiling of the camera.

These fish racks, of which a number were encountered, are built thus: ⟋ by slanting dams of rocks, sticks, etc.; they begin from the shore in a narrow, shallow part of the stream, and running down stream, meet in the center; at the end of each wing a huge rock is placed, with an iron spike embedded in it.

To the spikes a fyke-net is fastened, into which the eels are enmeshed as they are carried down by the current. The nets are set and watched at night, and require to be taken up and emptied every two hours.

The practice is illegal, and the racks are only built in secluded localities. Besides, they make very dangerous places for canoes or boats as the rush of water over the dam carries one along at a high rate of speed. Added to this is the danger of being impaled on the spikes, which, at low water, are about even with the surface.

Usually, one side or the other does not reach the bank, and the canoeist can diverge either way before entering the trap. The lines of foam and spray, sparkling ahead, also help to denote danger.

Not including these shallows, we ran on this day twelve rifts, including Mary and Sambo (channel to left of island), Ground Hog, Hay Cock and Fiddler's Elbow.

We were now, strictly speaking, in the Delaware valley. We left the "endless chain of mountains," when we ran down the rift, below Port Jervis, and rounded to at the mouth of the peaceful Neversink, or in the Indian tongue, "Mohaccomac" branch.

Years ago, before 1675, that branch of the Delaware tribe, known as the Minsimini, or Wolf tribe, roamed at will between these waters and the Forks at Easton. On the plains at these two points notable council fires were held. Here also is the terminus of the Upper Indian Path, reaching from Navesink to Minisink.

On our right, back from the river, ran the cliffs, eight hundred feet in height. The stage road to Water Gap winds at the very base, and the landscape is unsurpassed. The limestone soil is most excellent, and the region is noted for its agricultural products.

The early history of the valley we were now traveling, compared with its present state, forcibly calls to mind those lines of Bryant's—

> "Before these fields were shorn and tilled
> Full to the brim our rivers flowed;
> The melody of waters filled
> The fresh and boundless wood;
> And torrents dashed and rivulets played
> And fountains spouted in the shade."

We were told not to miss the falls of the Raymondskill, and were sorry that our time was too limited to enable us to take the wild tramp. Dingman's High Falls and the Silver Thread we also had to forego visiting.

Our intention at starting was to make Bushkill by evening, and, as it was one o'clock when we reached Dingman's Ferry, a stoppage of a couple of hours would throw us far back of our schedule. We were shown the long rift by a vigorous farmer-waterman, who became deeply interested in our craft.

He was very doubtful as to our ability to run the rift, and looked incredulous when we told him what we had accomplished.

"What did you do about 'Lackawax?'" he queried doubtingly.

"Ran it," sententiously answered Carter.

"In a pig's eye you did," he drawled out.

As we passed, he jumped into an unwieldly, high-sided row-boat, propelled by clumsy oars, having bent handles, working on tholes, and accompanied us to the head of the rift.

It was only an ordinary shallow stretch, with an eighteen-inch drop over the first ledge.

As usual, in taking a narrow channel, we went through Indian file, and our friend was pleased as we glided down like so many turtles without any mishap. He waved us a good-bye, and shouted a warning about Foul Rift as we passed out of hearing. At the end of the rift, broken stone piers told the tale of a freshet and a wrecked bridge.

The country about us, on both sides, we judged to be extremely wild. Large game abounds in the interior, and the river affords good bass fishing.

During the latter part of the afternoon we paddled through some long stretches of deep and rough water. The day had been perfect, and we felt in excellent spirits.

In running a succession of rapids I became separated from the rest, just being able to see their paddle blades flash in the sunlight as they approached the edge of some steep rift. Rounding a bend, I lost sight of them entirely, and landed at the foot of a meadow that began some feet above the river. Close by the cliffs, a cosy farm nestled.

Stretched at ease under the overhanging trees, I spent a very pleasant and restful hour. A soft breeze swept through the valley, and before me, in New Jersey, lay a fine, well-cultivated farm. Barns and buildings were strung along the river-bank, and a long, low country house was visible on the side of a commanding hill, the brow of which was reached by a series of natural terraces. To the left a plowman was busy turning furrows, and in the woods, lower down, the ringing sound of an axe was heard. As I meditated visions of a cold fall and winter, housed crops and marketed produce filled my mind. And then the farmer's season of ease, the daily duties, and the following quiet evenings before open fire-places and huge wood-fires. Not a bad picture, I think I hear you echoing.

I had waited long, and was beginning to get uneasy about the boys, thinking they might have taken another channel, when I saw a couple of canoes creeping down in the shadow of the fast departing day.

They proved to be captained by Cooper and Donnelly, who shortly landed near me.

The boys reported Allen's canoe as having sprung a leak, through a long split, probably received in the morning's accident. Carter had stopped with him to see what they could do with the fracture, and expected to catch up with us as soon as possible, so we dropped paddles and waited near a cooling spring that bubbled from the gravel.

Cooper, in nosing along shore, had fallen in with a fisherman and found in him an interesting talker. He had been a raft pilot at Lackawaxen dam, taking rafts through for twelve shillings each. He also sounded the warning about Foul Rift, although he said we could make it if we were careful.

For himself he said he hated the place, as it was swift and rocky. He almost met with an accident at one time while running the rift, unshipping a sweep in the worst place. Happily he recovered the unwieldly, but essential article, before the raft became unmanageable.

Carter and Allen soon joined us, having succeeded in repairing the broken *Werowance.*

The sun was now directly over the river course, and the last four miles were made with the annoyance of having Sol's rays directly in our eyes. This was bad for us, especially so on a strange part of the river. We had to depend mainly on the current floating us into the right channel.

We took three rifts thus handicapped, and it was slow work. We also narrowly escaped being swept down on a low hanging ferry guide-wire, which reached across the river at the head of one of the rifts.

We landed at the fishery, near a dark ravine, the wild mouth of the Bushkill creek. The town lay so far away, that on account of approaching darkness we decided not to visit it, but instead looked about for a camp site. We found ourselves on the arm of the famous Walpack bend, the ferry of the early settlers in this section. To the left was the Walpack Ridge. Close to the right shore arose a member of the Blue mountain range. Above us, the nearest railroad was at Port Jervis, below, at Water Gap. The country we found very thinly inhabited.

In Pennsylvania the damp wooded mountain-side gave no hope of a camp, so we turned our canoes to New Jersey.

Now, as in the time of the colonists, we found her ever ready to give shelter to the traveler. On a bluff, about fifteen feet above the water, we found a fine level for pitching our tents, and back and above us, on another slope, was a far-reaching wheat field. The lifting and carrying of duffle from the water's edge to the height was the only objectionable feature.

It was dark when we finished pitching tents, and we were tired. Camp-fires soon lit up the dark surroundings, and were reflected in the waters beneath.

Hungry mortals we, as we gathered around the evening meal, and the appetite each exhibited was an honest one, full of meaning.

While thus engaged we witnessed a grand sight, which will ever live in our memories. Directly opposite, rising from out the water's dark depths, towered a hemlock and pine-covered mountain cliff, the leafy effect in the dusk shading from dark green to black.

Above the cliff's edge, we first noticed a halo of light, which grew brighter as the moon ascended.

Then, clear cut against the dark blue sky, Luna's upper edge appeared, forming an enchanting background for the display of the feathery limbs and leafy tree tops on the brow of the rocky eminence. Slowly it mounted, until the whole display of interlaced treeforms was marked in bold relief on its brilliant face. As it passed higher into the heavens, the oblique rays of light lit up the hillside and were reflected in the current.

The scene was sublimely grand, and, musically, the current rippled below us:

How sweet the moonlight sleeps upon this bank!
Here we will sit and let the sounds of music
Creep in our ears: Soft stillness and the night
Become the touches of sweet harmony.

To add to the romance of the situation, the long-drawn cries of owls sounded in the forests, and katy-dids rasped about us.

The latter signify six weeks from frost, according to the accepted idea, but we imagined that we had slept in it on several occasions.

The fires burned low, and the boys were resting and sleeping. Looking out on the peaceful scene, as I lay on my cot, warmly banked by blankets, I could not help recalling a little bit of history, that tells how nearly two hundred and fifty years ago nigh this very spot, during an Indian uprising on the frontier of New Jersey, the family of Nicholas Cole was unexpectedly attacked, and its members murdered or carried off.

Upon investigation, the massacre was justified by the Indians on the ground that the hanging for murder of one of their Sachems, Wee-que-helah, had been without cause.

This is only one of many bloody scenes through which our country has passed. The valley of the Delaware, however, was noted for its continued peace during the exciting times of the early settlement of the three states on whose borders we were journeying. That the condition of affairs in this section, as they existed, was due to that truly good Quaker, William Penn, is undeniable, and the esteem in which he was held by the Delaware tribes is proof of the justice of his dealings with them.

CHAPTER 8.

An Indian Dream Legend.
The Blue Mountains.
Water Gap.
A Bit of Femininity.
Rock Formations.
Farming.
Ramsaysburg.
Music and Echoes.
A Handy Liquid.
Sweet Sleep.

"Each day is a little life."—*Lubbock*.

HE morning was well advanced when we turned out, and, consequently, we had late breakfast. The sun was a long time breaking through the foglike mist, which hung clinging to the mountains about us.

At breakfast Carter accused Allen of having made some wild statements and gyrations in his sleep, but could give no definite reasons for them beyond the fact that the dreamer appeared in great trepidation.

We came to the conclusion that owing to the historical associations of the surroundings the tired canoeist had had a vision of the curious Lenâpé legend *Amangachktiatmachque*, or Legend of the Big, Frightful Naked Bear.

This animal, of which even at that time there was a scarcity, had been hunted by the different tribes, and was immense in size and very ferocious. Its skin was bare, with the exception of a tuft of white hair on its back. The animal was, also, very fond of Indian meat, and the pursuer frequently became the pursued. When the tables were thus turned the native's only safety was in reaching water. The naked bear's olfactory nerve was well developed, but, as is usually the case with monstrosities, the acuteness of one part was offset by a corresponding dullness of another, in this instance by defective sight.

Its heart was so small an arrow could not enter it with certainty be the archer ever so skillful. The only sure method was to break the creature's back-bone. This, we conjectured, was the dreamer's object, hence his wild motions.

The sun's rays streamed directly into camp, drying our effects thoroughly. We gathered and packed duffle on the bluff, and then rolled it down to the canoes where the operation of stowing was performed. At ten o'clock we crossed the river, seeking the shade of the precipitous cliff. The sun heated the narrow channel unmercifully.

I must digress here to warn that any future cruiser, if in looking through these glassy waters to the river bed, he should see numerous white squares, strewn irregularly over the gravel, and wonder thereat, not to investigate if tempted so to do. No curious glacial formations are they; no relics of Indian handicraft; no mirrors of English fur-traders. They are simply camera plates, whose future usefulness had been impaired by damp wetness, the result of the accident below Milford.

For two and a half miles of our morning journey we did not advance at all, substantially retracing on another arm of the river, the route we had run the night before. After many twists and turns, during which evolutions we were on a down grade, we straightened out and commenced a tedious experience in rapids running, under a burning sun and against a head wind.

The water was very heavy and deep, with numerous cross currents.

We remarked some fine scenery above Water Gap. Far ahead of us, in the distance, enveloped in a blue mist, could be seen the bold ranges of the Blue mountains, with their peaks and gaps.

> " 'Tis distance lends enchantment to the view,
> And robes the mountain in its azure hue!"

Most noticeable were the peaks, Minsi and Tammany, which form the famed water gate through which the river rushes, from thenceforth to flow through an important farming and grazing district, irrigated by innumerable streams, whose charming, peaceful valleys afford unsurpassed facilities for market gardening.

We passed a little raft on its way to Water Gap. The owners were having a tedious experience with the head wind and the numerous shoals.

Reaching the landing at the grove about half-past one o'clock, we hauled canoes out on the sandy shore and went up into town.

Cooper, who was ahead of us, had gone down the next rift. We expected him to join us in the town. In this we were disappointed, as he staid below taking photographs until we joined him.

At the Delaware House we had lunch, and then went shopping for provisions; and thereby hangs a tale.

From necessity our party had formed no Academe, such as Shakespeare depicts in *Love's Labor's Lost*. To my knowledge none had been tied by silken bands, or left a love-lorn maid at home. Still a hard cruise amidst many trials, with only male companionship, gives wonderful acuteness to that longing for women's faces, if the eye is at all susceptible to those daintier charms.

It is no wonder then, that when we sun-burned river travelers came across a charming bit of womanhood in the confectionery at the foot of the mountain road, we became most deferential and polite.

The pretty miss' cream-colored dress, loosely gathered in careless folds, enhancing a pair of brown eyes and wavy-like hair, proved an irresistible combination, suggestive of Johnson's delicately-turned verse.

As a compliment, cream was purchased where, in truth, the aromatic pipe would have been preferable.

After making purchases, we took a walk up the mountain path to the Kittatinny and Mountain Hotels, and stopped at the Glen and Bazaar.

At the latter place the proprietor was much interested in our trip, and deprecated our running Foul Rift. He told us he was acquainted with young Mr. Leiper, of Philadelphia, who was drowned in the rift last July.

He said the channel was on the Pennsylvania side, but would not take the responsibility of further instructing us.

During the morning we remarked the heat, even upon the water when we were running against the wind. In town it was unbearable. We learned that the east was experiencing a hot wave that had been predicted several days previously.

We joined Carter at the hotel, and then returned to the boats. The place at which we stopped was the upper landing, where a side wheel steamer lay. We were informed that during the season she plied back and forth to and above the railroad bridge. Between the upper landing and the Mountain House wharf is a shallow rift. Between this rift and the Gap another steamer carries sightseers.

The sun was shining bright and strong, but Mount Minsi cast a grateful shadow, which we sought. Mount Tammany (from Tamenend, the noted Delaware chieftain, who dealt with Penn), bold and rocky, appeared ahead, outlined against a perfectly clear sky.

Numerous fishing parties and "girling" canoes clotted the placid o'ershadowed waters. The black bass were biting freely.

As we floated down with the current the solid front of mountain began to show irregular outlines. A few strokes of the paddles and we found our course again close to the base of these lofty, silent sentinel peaks.

Just before entering the rift below the Gap, we noticed on the down stream side of the right-hand cliff, the profile of a man's face, plainly marked. To heighten the effect a bush at the chin formed a realistic goatee.

The Blue mountains at this point are known as the Shawangunk in New York and New Jersey, and as the Kittatinny in Pennsylvania. The elevation at the Water Gap is 1,479 feet above the sea level.

The geological formations prominently exposed, as we proceeded, were sand and limestone soils, and trap rock. Slate also abounds, and a most successful quarry is located at Water Gap. Further down the river, below Easton, granite is quarried in commercial quantities.

The cultivated and tillable soil every where in this region is formed from decayed rock. The Oriskany sandstone and the magnesian limestone readily disintegrate, and form rich and productive soils, supplying phosphoric acid and potash in abundance. The climate, rainfall and natural drainage are combinations bound to be appreciated by those seeking profitable farms, and the percentage of recovered arable lands has greatly increased.

Below Water Gap the country began to spread out, and the river showed many shallows.

We had plenty of excitement as we took one rift after another until sun-down. We passed numerous islands above and below Water Gap, and we kept mostly to the Jersey channel. During low water the best course must be selected from the many that present themselves, and one need not expect to get along without grounding.

Below Portland we entered a winding and swift rift in which Carter was hung up, without any serious mishap, however.

It was dusk when we found a camp site, at Ramsaysburg, two miles above Manunka Chunk.

The site selected was at the edge of a commanding bluff, the termination of an extensive Jersey farm. Not far up stream a ferry was established.

It was indeed a camp much welcomed by all hands. The day had been intolerably hot, and we had battled with a head wind until sundown. Besides making about twenty-five miles, we had had the mountain climb at the Gap, which in itself was hard on muscles unused to the work.

The *Nahiwi* was hauled bodily up the bluff and unpacked in camp for convenience, and as a labor-saving expedient.

As the shades of night were falling our camp was completed, and moonlight beamed upon us as we sat down to a hearty dinner of steak, eggs, potatoes and coffee.

The night was clear and warm, and the moon's soft light over the rolling hills and wide expanse of water formed withal a pleasing picture for the memory.

From afar, on the still night breezes and echoing in the valley, came strains of music o'er the quiet waters. The receding slopes about us caught up the swelling tones, bearing them onward, until the sounds died away in the night like the distant hush of a purling stream.

'Twas undoubtedly such an incident as this that evoked the following verse from Moore—

> "How sweet the answer Echo makes,
> To music at night
> When roused by lute or harp, she wakes,
> And far away o'er lawns and lakes,
> Goes answering light."

From our vantage point above the stream we listened to the sounds—sweet recollections of home.

We built a snug camp-fire for comradeship and enjoyed it until late, for rest and refreshment to mind and body are wonderful stimulants.

We had two invalids in camp, Cooper nursing a sprained wrist, and Donnelly a bad cold. Jamaica rum was the antidote for both ailments. It was applied externally as a liniment in the former case, by inhalation in the latter.

The joke of the evening was an incident that happened at Water Gap. The Quartermaster had fallen into the habit of calling Carter, "Dad," and in the course of conversation at the hotel, made use of the appellation in the hearing of a third party, who earnestly inquired if such really was the case.

We were out of the mountain mists and dews at last, and to-morrow we could look for a clear morning much earlier than usual.

To-morrow, too—and it was discussed about the camp-fire—we would know whether we were to continue to Trenton as a party, or break up on the other side of Big Foul.

We turned in with assurances of a hearty sleep, possibly, however, to be disturbed with visions of artistically carved canoe bottoms and frantic struggles in a resistless, rock-strewn tide.

CHAPTER 9.

A Clear Morning.
We Find a Channel.
Belvidere.
Foul Rift.
The Second Accident.
Drowning of a Canoeist.
Phillipsburg and Easton.
Above Carpenterville.
A Country Hotel.

Row, brothers, row! the stream runs fast,
The rapids are near and the daylight's past!
"Canadian Boat Song,"—*Moore.*

E WERE all out at six o'clock, in time to see the sun rise, a sight strange to us, who had been so long in the misty Highlands.

For the first time in a week our camp equipments were dry. Not a particle of dew had fallen.

As early as eight o'clock canoes were packed, and, breakfast over, we pushed away from our night's camp, with bright prospects of a pleasant day.

Below Manunka Chunk we saw some distance ahead a series of islands, and were in doubt as to the proper channel to take. Running ashore, I stopped at a house on the bank to ascertain the lay of the land. In the door-yard I met an elderly lady, of whom I inquired if our party could, with safety, follow the left shore.

"No, sir," she answered, with a rising inflection.

"The channel, then, is on the right?" I interrogated.

"Yes," she replied as before, but added, hastily, "You can't get down there. The rifts are ahead of you."

"Thank you," I replied, "That is just what we wanted to know."

Our informant was right. We found plenty of rifts, and bad ones, too, some nineteen to Raubville, and they were deep, swift and rough. Notably so were Long Rift and Buttermilk Rift, above Belvidere.

On our way we passed several fishing parties, and each had some particularly horrible phase of Foul Rift to pound into our ears "free, gratis, for nothing." And I believe if we had not firmly intended to pass through at any cost, we would have been scared into avoiding this spot before even seeing it.

One, a ferryman, wanted to know if the fate of one canoeist was not enough to make us afraid of it, without wanting to take a personal risk.

Carter, laconically, answered his question by asking another—namely, if he was afraid to go to bed.

Laughing and catching the point, he said "no," and wished us a safe passage.

Just above Belvidere our photographer got a pretty picture of the yet distant town with its wild background.

Another picture taken, an ideal subject for a landscape painting, was a water-wheel, standing alone in a wild and rocky glen back of the river. The buildings had been carried away by flood, and only the wrecked wheel remained.

We ran in at the mouth of Pequest creek at ten o'clock, and went ashore to send telegrams and letters, and to express a lot of undeveloped plates.

In the town we heard nothing but Foul Rift, and how dangerous and swift it was.

Of course we could pardon the natives, as there is considerable rivalry existing between them and the people of Lambertville as to the honor of the worst rift on the river, Wells' Falls being upheld by the Lambertvillians as even the more dangerous of the two places.

Foul Rift is, without doubt, a bad place to encounter, and always has been. Proude's *History of Pennsylvania*, published in 1798, calls it by the same name on the map issued with Vol. I. Smith's *History of New Jersey*, 1765, says:

"The Delaware river, from the head of Cushietunk, though not obstructed with falls, has not been improved to any inland navigation, by reason of the thinness of the settlements that way. From Cushietunk (Cochecton) to Trenton Falls, are fourteen considerable rifts, yet all passable in the long, flat boats used in the navigation of these parts, some carrying 500 or 600 bushels of wheat. The greatest number of rifts are from Easton downward, and those fourteen miles above Easton, another just below Wells' Ferry, and that at Trenton are the worst. The boats seldom come down but with freshes, especially from the Minnisinks."

The rift fourteen miles above Easton is, undoubtedly, Foul Rift. The boats mentioned were somewhat on the style of the Durham boats, forty or fifty feet long and seven feet wide, built of heavy planking, and drawing about twenty inches of water. The up-river ferry scows are built with about these dimensions even to-day.

In the rift the limestone ledges and the scattered limestone rocks, with their serrated edges and deep pot holes, over which the current sweeps and churns rapidly and loudly, are constant sources of danger.

The limestone does not wear smooth by the action of the water, but breaks in jagged layers, leaving sharp angles, and points that cut like knives.

Pushing away from the raft to which we had tied, we floated down with the stream, each one baring for the fray, arms tanned to the shoulders.

We had every confidence in our craft, and our duffle was packed without danger of shifting—we had paid marked attention to that with each article stowed, in the early morning.

We would also see whether the experience gained in rifts above amounted to anything at a pinch.

At 11:07, with Carter in the lead, we entered Little Foul at the edge of a bend. At the foot of the incline we straightened out and passed into the eddy above the Big Rift.

We could hear in the distance the old familiar sound we had oft listened for to designate either a rift or fall, but in this instance it sounded with greater volume than usual.

"Do you hear it, Hoff?" asked Carter, as the *Nahiwi* ran alongside.

"Yes, and see it, too," I answered, for thickly to the left lay sentinel rocks high in air, against which the current broke in angry spray, covering the shore with perpetual moisture.

Truly the channel was "to Pennsylvania," and exceedingly narrow.

Carter and I were swept onward in safety, and were steering for the last drop over which the current boiled and seethed, when to me it seemed as if his canoe would be carried down on a ragged rock lying fairly in the channel.

If so, this would throw him across the narrow opening, and I would certainly foul him. Pointing my canoe close to a gravel formation, jutting down stream, I was preparing to jump, when I saw the *Zerlina* swing clear, the force of the water against the rock helping her past in safety.

I headed for the current again, but too late to pass the end of the bar, which was strewn with rocks, and collided with a sharp one, striking on the left forward quarter. The force caused the point of rock to go through the garboard-streak like an axe, and water commenced to leak through the break. So clean was the cut and so great the speed that the canoe was not deflected from her course, nor the jar noticed.

I took the last drop and landed at 11:20 with a great deal of water shipped.

Allen and Donnelly came through with plenty of water aboard, having struck only at the last ledge. With the exception of being hung up on a rock at the entrance, Cooper was all right.

And so we ran this *bête noir* of the Delaware river raftsmen.

The length of the incline is about a mile and a half. Therefore the rate of the canoe's speed was not so great. The course was rock-strewn and rough, but still no worse than the rift at Masthope, where in places the current is quicker than here. I remember striking a rock in the Masthope rift, hitting squarely on the keel with such force as to be thrown or slid completely over it. Had the canoe drawn half an inch more water she would have been a wreck.

Foul Rift is bad for rafts on two accounts, first, the sharp bend in approaching it; and second, the rocks on the Jersey side.

For amateur canoeists, starting in at Port Jervis, or at Water Gap, with no previous experience, it is dangerous, and had better be avoided, as had Wells' Falls. For a canoeman fresh from the trying school below Hancock, it should have no terrors. A scow or batteau could not get through when the water is low without striking. On a full river or fresh it could be done easily. In fact, the people exaggerate its dangers from hearsay. In most cases, where the natives have to depend on their own knowledge for the name, location, or channel, unless they be fishermen, or follow rafting, the information is not of much assistance.

A very sad accident happened here on the tenth of July, during the present year, when Samuel Leiper, a young Philadelphia canoeist, and press correspondent, was drowned. He, in company with three others, started from Water Gap, bound on a cruise in search of health and recreation. The four canoeists traveled in two canvas canoes, and went all right until they attempted Foul Rift, where they capsized. All were rescued but Mr. Leiper, who attempted to swim ashore. He was swept down on a rock and killed.

Two of the party, Messrs. Williams and Johnson, had made the trip from Port Jervis the year before, having stopped at Park Island, on that occasion, and were confident of repeating it successfully.

The real danger lay not in the river, so much as in the men traveling two in a boat, which should not be done under any circumstances. In this instance, not only did this disadvantage exist, but the two men were amateurs, and one was lame. Everything was therefore against the feat being accomplished safely.

This is one of the rare instances of the drowning of a canoeist, and while very deplorable, was almost to be expected, unless the parties bore charmed lives. Trusting to luck does not carry one through everything.

While repairing the broken *Nahiwi*, we had a conversation with a fisherman named Dickey, who said he had been watching for us every day, as he had been told by his brother that we were on our way down.

He told us he had seen almost every canoeing party that had run the falls, and mentioned several with whom we were familiar. He slyly remarked that usually some of the boats were hauled up for repairs before proceeding.

Further down, on the Pennsylvania bank, lay the *Wanderer*, one of the canoes abandoned by the Philadelphia cruisers. Over her floated a couple of American flags.

Nearby we met Samuel Snyder, of Easton, who, with Mr. Dickey, was instrumental in recovering the body of the drowned canoeist, and in rescuing the other members of the ill-fated party.

We landed on a sand bank at the foot of the rift, hardby a pretty grove of larches, while Cooper photographed the surroundings, and also a point of the limestone formation half way down the rift.

After resting we continued our trip, running Cape Bush, Bush, Little Bush, Martin's, and Smalley rifts, getting plenty of vigorous exercise. The twists in the channels were constant revelations, and although we started in a rift on the Jersey shore, it were wonderful if we had not been to the Pennsylvania shore and back again in traversing its length.

At Brainerd's we sought shelter from the heat of the sun, in a grove above the railroad bridge. Our rest was made doubly restful by the unexpected arrival of a pitcher of milk and some large home-made ginger cakes, obtained at a nearby farm-house.

An hour later we reached Phillipsburg and Easton, twin cities on the heights, after meeting with some rough falls above, especially at Sandt's Eddy. Here we stopped awhile to rest, as we had plenty of time to make Raubville before nightfall.

Phillipsburg in New Jersey and Easton in Pennsylvania are representative cities of the two states. The former is conspicuous for its extensive blast furnaces and manufactories, and the traffic incident to its being the terminus of the Morris canal, and the central shipping and transfer point for coal and iron products, through the medium of the Lehigh Valley and the Belvidere Division Railroads.

> "From the hundred chimneys of the village,
> Like the afreet in the Arabian story, smoky columns
> Tower aloft in the air of amber."

Easton, with Lafayette College, its canal and railroad facilities and rich agricultural districts, ranks with the representative cities of the state.

Habit is strong with us. At noon, October 10th, 1887, I left Phillipsburg for a cruise down to Trenton. On that occasion I paddled under the railroad bridge, close to the right bank, there not being sufficient water over the dam. To-day, as we continued, I took the same course. Carter, Allen, Cooper and Donnelly went through the shute.

The water below was rough and deep, as it flowed through a cut formed by a high bank on the right, and the railroad embankment on the left. Here a number of lads, in swimming, gave chase to our canoes, their lithe bodies cutting the water quickly, in their efforts to distance the paddle.

The waning afternoon was pleasant, affording a grateful change from the heat in which we had been paddling. We had ample time to make camp, and were in no particular hurry, floating downward, scarcely a breeze ruffling the water.

Above Carpenterville the inland country ahead, terminating in the far distance in a series of elevations and depressions, formed a companion to the exquisite picture which we beheld at the junction of the Neversink, and about Port Jervis. The water from now on we noticed was not as clear as above Easton, being foul with coal and sewage. It takes seven miles for a stream to purify itself, and not until it gets below Raubville is the water clean again.

The river was quite wide, and we were on the crest of an incline that ended in a noisy rush, caused by a dam that extended half way to the Pennsylvania shore.

We were in a quandary regarding a camping spot. so Donnelly went ashore to ascertain about hotels. A couple of our party had wet blankets and did not care to make camp, as the night was likely to prove cool. Whilst waiting for the Quartermaster, we stopped in an eddy back of some exposed rocks in mid-stream. In the water the inverted shadows of surrounding objects appeared as clear cut as the original outlines against the perfect sky.

Presently our attention was attracted, by the angry barking of dogs, to the bank on which our courier had landed. We at once beheld Donnelly backing down a crooked pathway with a stick in either hand, keeping at bay a pack of mongrel curs. Jumping into his canoe he pushed off hastily, leaving some disappointed canines howling for fresh meat.

We learned that at this season there were no hotel accommodations to be had at Carpenterville, but that across the river, at Raubville, we could stop at the Delaware House. As it was fast falling night, we decided to stop for supper and breakfast, and to make an early start in the morning.

We completed a thirty-three mile paddle by running in the dusk the dam and rift before mentioned, and hauling the boats up in front of "ye hostelrie."

Saturday night at a country hotel is not without its interesting features. The week's work over, the farmers from the country-side gather to discuss crops, horses and politics. On this occasion the latter subject received a stimulant in the shape of the high sheriff, who had stopped on his way home from Doylestown, the county seat of Bucks county.

It was late at night before the ferry to the Jersey shore ceased from business. But we had sought our welcome rest in "tired Nature's sweet restorer—balmy Sleep!"

CHAPTER 10.

Tricks of a Camera.
Some Places of Interest.
Ringing Rocks.
Religious Sects.
Frenchtown.
God's Country.
At Erwinna.
Lambertville.
Falls to Tide-Water.
Welcomed Home.
Washington's Crossing.
Local History.
The Moon Once More.
Exeunt.

The sun is down and time gone by
The stars are twinkling in the sky,
Nor torch nor taper longer may
Eke out a blythe but stinted day;
The hours have passed with stealthy flight
We needs must part; good night, good night!
—*Joanna Baillie.*

WE HAD an early breakfast served, and made the start at eight o'clock. Cooper photographed our last camp on the cruise, and it was fun to see the stable boy and man of all work pose with broom and rake. Their attitudes may have been perfect and unstrained, but they will never be any the wiser, for they were "not in it." A camera is a "wery deceivin' creetur," it may be looking squarely at you and yet won't see you at all.

Forty-four miles to Trenton. Would we make it to-day? Cooper said "yes," and Donnelly, "no."

We waited to see.

The sky was slightly clouded, and the country on this Sunday morning seemed so quiet and entirely different from that of a week ago, when we floated through rifts and down placid pools, enjoying the scenery as it lay spread out before us.

This day we encountered innumerable rifts and long stretches of shallows. During the morning we left behind us Pincher's Point, a bass fishing locality, Warren, Upper Black's Eddy, where the deep waters are continually bub-

131

bling and eddying for a considerable distance; Brougher's, or Hog-Back Island, yielding cobblestone on the upper and sand on the lower end; Reiglesville, with its curious rift and rocks and the dam; Durham Furnace, a portion of the extensive Cooper & Hewitt iron plant, and then Milford. Across the river, at the latter place, runs the canal, and near the road is a canal-boat yard, with powerful cribs or jacks for bending the heavy bow timbers.

Up on the mountains of Pennsylvania a curious phenomenon exists, known as the Ringing Rocks, a collection of metallic boulders that emit ringing and even musical combinations of sounds upon being struck. Wonderful to relate, there is not a tradition as to how they came there. They present to the eye an aggregation a couple of acres in extent, in the midst of the cultivated mountain plateau.

Further inland the religious sects, known as Dunkards, Moravians and Mennonites, have their social colonies, and each is well known in the large towns adjacent.

At twelve o'clock we reached Frenchtown and stopped for dinner, and it was after one o'clock when we resumed paddling. Our way lay through a comparatively flat country, famed for its crops of corn, wheat, rye and potatoes. But not until you reach Trenton do you strike the real low country.

The districts bordering on the Delaware fall into three classes, the Highlands, from Hancock to Port Jervis; the Delaware valleys, of which there are several from Port Jervis to Trenton, and the lowlands from Trenton to Delaware Bay.

Each district has its peculiar value. The timber lands belonging to the first district are very important indeed, the scarcity of lumber and the destruction of forests being vigorously discussed in economic journals. The agricultural districts of the second are the life and stay of our manufacturing towns. And the cranberry, charcoal, vineyard and peach sections of the third are all well known and important.

A noticeable fact concerning the section through which we were traveling was that the river villages of any importance center about some milling industry, the motive power for which was obtained by the construction of temporary dams, race-ways or canal weirs. These prosperous hamlets were mostly noticed on the New York and New Jersey shores, where some inland stream was utilized, or where dams running to the center of the Delaware had been constructed.

On the Pennsylvania shore we failed to see these dams, and only saw two or three mills. The reason for this is the lack of legislation in the big state legalizing the construction of dams. This is very short-sighted policy, as a few low dams, with long race-ways, placed in the river to control the power for manufacturing purposes, would in a few years, with its present start and possibilities, make the Delaware valley the rival of the far-famed Merrimac, Passaic and Ohio valleys.

We shot through Bull's Island (Raven Rock) dam, and down the rapids at three o'clock, passing Point Pleasant. At the latter place, during an August freshet, a store and dwelling were swept from their foundations, bringing up in pieces at Penn's Manor, below Trenton.

Before reaching this place, we had a tedious experience among the islands and shoals between Erwinna and Tumble, where it was necessary to get out and wade for some distance. Those of our party who passed to the right of the island found deeper water. The channel on the Jersey side is close to the island.

Above Lambertville we passed Eagle and Hendricks Islands, with their grassy camping spots, and Carter regaled us with camp experiences from 1883 to within a few years of the present time. The channel at these places will be found on the left-hand side.

We reached Lambertville, sixteen miles above Trenton, at five o'clock, and it was a question for debate whether we should camp on one of the many pleasing slopes, or continue homeward.

The question, however, was decided for us in a most delightful manner. On going under the bridge, we saw ahead of us a crowd of Park Island canoeists at the canal lock, waiting to welcome, feed, and escort home five proud but tired cruisers. Hand-shakings, congratulations, and good-cheer infused new strength, and, of course, we decided to go on with the boys.

It was fast falling dusk, and after Wells' Falls come the Bucktails, Titusville rift, Scudder's Falls, and Park Island rift, so, as all the other craft were in the canal, we decided to carry thither.

Weils' Falls is caused by the present dam. It is a bad place at low water, on account of the rocks below the opening forming a treacherous foamer.

Scudder's Falls have a narrow shute through the dam, and is only a drop and a rough race.

The other places mentioned are only ordinary rifts, and traveling down the left side of the river will take you through them all. Trenton Falls has the channel right in the center, all the way through. It is winding. however, and the first part takes you close to a long gravel bar on the left-hand side.

Many hands make light work, and the carry was soon completed. Chatting and rehearsing incidents, wonders and escapes of the trip, and breaking bread with our escorts, in some twenty canoes, we invaded the quiet vale and left much wonderment in our wake.

It was growing dark when we carried to the river and floated down past Washington's Crossing.

Back in a grassy hollow nestled the old-fashioned, shingle-covered house, of hewn timbers and curved gables, that sheltered General Washington and his aides on that memorable Christmas eve, 1776, when the Continental army crossed the river, amid the floating ice, and landed on New Jersey soil. Their march to Trenton by the Pennington road and the capture of the Hessian troops are incidents that have been vividly recalled by recent historical celebrations.

The house, erected about ten years prior to the revolution, is a fitting picture of "ye olden colonial tymmes," and bears the scars of many winters. Inside, over the open fireplace, the wooden mantle shows curious poker tracings, and a deep hole in the wall tells the tale of pistol practice at short range, spotting the ace.

Across in Pennsylvania, at the end of the gravel bar, where the old ferry road used to run, is the point from which the crossing was made. The ferry, known as McKenty's ferry, connected with the road on the Jersey shore, which then ran to the river at a point near where the old house stands.

The Pennsylvania road ended above the present toll bridge, about in front of Dr. Griffith's residence. Later a toll bridge was erected lower down, and the roads on both sides extended to connect with it. Thus traces of the ferry were destroyed.

To mark the original spot, the Bucks County Historical Society contemplated erecting a fifteen-dollar monument, but so much fun was made of the amount appropriated that nothing further has been done, at this writing, than to haul stones for the foundation, which stones still lay piled near the spot.

When the first toll-bridge was built a Quaker painter executed two paintings of Washington and his favorite steed, nailing one at each end of the bridge.

When the bridge was destroyed by a freshet, years ago, one picture was taken possession of by Landlord Jamieson, of Taylorsville, and the other fell into the hands of the proprietor of the Washington's Crossing hotel. The former was presented to the Historical Society of Pennsylvania, while the latter adorns the bar of the hostelrie on the Jersey side. There are many other incidents connected with the surroundings, the relation of which with more detail has been reserved for another part of this book.

As we journeyed on our old friend the moon came up full and grand from the peaceful hillside, making for us a bright pathway as we drifted down to Park Island, the home of the Trenton canoeists.

Here some of the party stopped at the Club house, and others went on, bound for "Home, Sweet Home!"

And so ended a charming vacation cruise, whose associations we shall ever recall with pleasure.

And, replete with Nature's varied phases and influences as was the time we passed, as we mused one and all, reëchoed with Shakespeare:

> "And this our life, exempt from public haunt,
> Finds tongues in trees, books in the running brook,
> Sermons in stones, and good in everything."

The End—Good Night.

APPENDIX 1.

REMARKS.

SOME time ago, while engaged in collaborating an historical sketch for a local paper, the author necessarily engaged in an extended research of acknowledged authorities, including such local treatises as Smith's *History of New Jersey*, 1765; Proude's *History of Pennsylvania*, 1798; *New York Gazeteer*, Tuttle's *Physical Man*, and, through the courtesy of the State Librarian of New Jersey, Col. Morris Hamilton, Brinton's *Aboriginal American Literature*, Vol. V., ("The Lenâpé and their Legends").

The reading, outside of the matter in hand at that time, proved very interesting, especially to one living in so historical a spot as is the vicinage of Trenton.

The settlement of the country, the Indians of the earlier periods, the acquisition of their lands, and other numerous details of our own unique history are such, that, once read, they are never entirely forgotten. It is no wonder then that in following up the incidents narrated in this volume, the author was forcibly impressed with the fact that the subject in hand from its local connections would warrant the introduction of a great many interesting passages pertaining to the early settlement. It was then suggested that the digression necessary would, at times, inconvenience the reader desiring to use the work as a book of reference—its main excuse for appearing.

To overcome this, and still give the pith of the historical happenings in sequence, the following concise presentation of "A Little Bit of History" was decided upon.

It is sincerely hoped that the perusal will give pleasure as well as instruction, inasmuch as the tendency of this busy age is to overlook those important incidents to which we, as a progressive nation, are so much indebted.

THE AUTHOR.

TRENTON, N. J., December 1st, 1892.

A LITTLE BIT OF HISTORY.

A Little Bit of History.

THE territory comprised by the Middle Atlantic States has always been intimately associated with the early history of our country.

The discovery of the Bahama Islands by Columbus in October, 1492; the landing of Vespucci in the Caribbees, and his further discoveries in the year 1501, through which this continent obtained its present name, though of vital importance in opening the way to the knowledge of a vast country hitherto unknown to the people of the Old World, did not receive such recognition from the powers benefited by these possessions as one would suppose. Still it was through the proclamations of these discoveries that Henry the Seventh, of England, was induced to charge an expedition for the discovery of lands in higher latitudes.

This expedition was under Sebastian Cabot, a Venetian explorer, who, in the year 1497, discovered and made a map of the country bordering on the ocean from Greenland to Florida. Possession was taken in the name of the crown of England, and the land, being waste and uncultivated, was, under the existing laws of nations, annexed and claimed by the English.

The English did not remain long in ignorance of the value of these new acquisitions. In the year 1584, a company of merchants, with Sir Walter Raleigh at the head, obtained a charter from Queen Elizabeth, of England, for making a settlement in America of "Virginia Territory," the habitable domain of the British possession as marked out by Cabot.

In rapid succession, history points to the discovery of Delaware bay and river, Hudson river, Chesapeake bay and Susquehanna river.

It was by the settlement of the lands along these rivers that the true character of the country was learned, and it is to the territory along the first of these streams that we will turn our attention.

To the Dutch East India Company belongs the honor of the discovery, in the year 1606, of South river.

Through their agent, Henry Hudson, an Englishman, this stream and the North (or Hudson) river were discovered and explored, with the result that the country was settled in the name of the Dutch, and called New Netherlands. News of this settlement reaching England the territory was claimed by the original proprietors, who compelled the Dutch to surrender their titles and lands.

By this reversion of rights we now have New York, in honor of James, Duke of York, and New Jersey, named by Sir George Carteret, whose family came from the Isle of Jersey.

The grants for these lands were conveyed to the proprietors in the year 1664, by King Charles the Second. It was not until 1681 that letters patent were granted William Penn, covering that tract of land lying "north of Maryland; bounded on the east by Delaware river; and on the west limited as Maryland and northward as far as plantable," from which letters we have the State of Pennsylvania.

Regarding the present name of Delaware, by which the historic stream and sheltering bay is known, history chronicles the fact that the South river, of the Dutch, was named as a compliment to the memory of Lord Delaware, who died at sea while voyaging to the Virginia Colony in the year 1618. The river, to Trenton and above, was called Charles river at first, while from Easton the Dutch bestowed upon it the name Viskill. By slow stages the stream from its source became known as the Delaware river.

So much for English history.

The very fact of a recital of the conditions governing the early settlement of the states mentioned, presupposes a consideration of previous Indian history. Possibly the latter possesses for all of us the most interesting features, en wrapped as it is, even at this day, in mystery.

To the question, "Who were the original discoverers of the new continent?" we must undoubtedly answer "The North American Indians, as they were known to the Old World." Previous to that, as the Spaniard queries—"*Quien Sabe?*"

The landing of Columbus was made in the presence of a strange people, whose language and mode of life was regarded with wonder by the Spaniards, who called them Indians, from the West Indies, the name given to all the first Spanish possessions in America, in contradistinction to "East Indies."

Vespucci in the Caribbees and Cabot at New Foundland encountered bands of natives each peculiar to the several sections of country discovered.

The Spaniards found the natives very simple, of a low order—possessing little intelligence, a crude language, and much superstition. They lived, too, in the most primitive manner. At all events, the statements of the discoverers and explorers upon their return home convey these opinions.

That they were grossly wrong in many respects is well known at the present day. The enlightenment of the early Indian tribes of this continent—their history, beliefs and traditions—only became partly known as late as the eighteenth century, and to-day the tangled skein is as yet unraveled.

The Indian opinion of the early Spanish and English people, who drove them from their land, we well know, for the hostile attitude of our western tribes to-day is an evidence that the injustice and imposition begun centuries ago still rankles. Weakened and surrounded though they are, they are living examples of the well-worn saying—"An Indian never forgets."

> "They linger yet,
> Avengers of their native land."

The time is not far off when the effects of whiskey, and the white man's avarice and vices, can be pointed at as having wiped a nation from the face of its rightful possession.

A detailed comparison of the inhabitants of the Old and New Worlds of the fifteenth century would prove of great interest from a scientific, physical and geographical standpoint. In the first place, the arts, science and literature of the European provinces had been slowly progressing for centuries under the most favorable conditions. In the New America, for how long? The answer is even to-day a conjecture.

Whence came the North American nomadic population? is a hard question to answer, to such an extent do different authorities conflict.

Thousands of people inhabited the continent when the Spaniards came. They had been living, migrating and accumulating knowledge long enough to have perfected the arts as far as they were needed for actual use. Their historical recollections, legends or traditions, like those of the Romans of old, were retained in chants and ceremonies, which were handed down from parent to children. Their literature was complete and concise, though to what extent we have no means of knowing, other than those afforded by incomplete records and long established oral rites.

The Spaniards claimed that the Indians knew nothing of their origin or ancestors, simply pointing to the sky when questioned regarding the former, and to the south as the abode of the latter. That the history of their forefathers was better understood by themselves than was claimed, is shown from the facts contained in the Indian records of late years, which consistently state that their ancestors came from the North and West. That they came from the North is proven by the fact that they were no strangers to cold—defying the coldest and bitterest weather. That they came from the West is known from their statement when driven from the colonies by the action of the whites—"They would return to the lands from whence they came."

Historians pretty generally agree that the country discovered by Columbus had been settled in the extreme North and West, 2,000 years B.C. The most plausible theory of such settlement is that wandering Aryan tribes from the Asiatic realm reached the main land by crossing Behring Straits on the Aleutian Isles, which in the early stages of history may have provided a continuous communication by land.

The sub-tribes in America, through migrations and otherwise, no doubt founded the nations as they are known to us to-day, viz., Eskimos, Aztecs, Incas, and lastly, the American Indians. And it is in connection with this latter tribe that we consider the settlement of the Delaware valley.

Discoveries had been made and possession taken right and left by foreign powers, with total disregard to the rights of the tribes occupying the new territory, but it was not until the year 1627 that history began to deal with the original owners of the continent—the Indians. In this year, nine years after the discovery of South river, the first recognition of the rights of the aboriginal settlers was when the Swedes purchased from them the country lying on both sides of the Delaware from Cape Henlopen (Paradise Point) to the falls now known as Trenton Falls. The river they called "New Swedesland stream."

Following the precedent established, further acquisitions of land embracing New Jersey, New York and Pennsylvania were made by purchase from the confederation known as the Five Nations.

It was on account of the equitable and just purchase from the rightful owners, even after the proprietary grants from the owners, that the State of Pennsylvania, through William Penn enjoyed the immunity from that Indian distrust which was so marked in those other sections seized and usurped by the early settlers.

> "On just and fairest terms the land is gain'd;
> No force of arms has any right obtain'd.
> 'Tis here, without the use of arms, alone,
> The blest inhabitant enjoys his own:
> Here many, to their wish, in peace enjoy
> Their happy lots; and nothing doth annoy.
> But sad New England's different conduct show'd
> What dire effects from injured Indians flow'd."

The Indian history relating to the territory embraced in the three states aforesaid, enables us to gain an insight into the conditions of the country and its inhabitants before the usurpation and final total possession by the whites. It is to the early English writers and missionaries that we are indebted for the preservation of the little now known of the Indians of America, their traditions and literature. Our own historians have perfected by all means possible such records of the savage era as have been left them. But the rapid extinction, caused by disease and forced migration from the first colonial possessions, has left an incompleteness of detail and ground-work for study the want of which has mainly been supplied by that most indefinite of all processes—theory.

Historical traditions from the most authentic sources establish the theory that the whole country contained scattered tribes of savages, each tribe being known as a nation with a head chief, king, or sachem. The legends of these different nations, interesting and quaint as they certainly are, disagree emphatically with each other in vital points. We can thus see the doubt and perplexity attendant upon the correct presentations of such records. That the tribes and confederacies had been at war with one another for an indefinite period, is well known by our own writers, from the chronicles of our own times. But that their war-like proclivities were aggravated by the whites cannot be disputed.

The territory inhabited and controlled by these tribes and alliances stretched from the Atlantic coast to the Rocky mountains; from the lakes to Georgia; even to the country north of New Foundland. To treat of the Indians, in connection with this work, brings us directly into contact with that tribe of the Five Nations, calling themselves the Grandfathers of Nation—the Lenni Lenâpé—the original Delaware Indians of present history. This nation claimed the totem symbolic of the legendary tortoise that supported the tribe on its back and saved it at the time of the flood. This legend, it will be noted, corresponds with the Brahmin legend of former times.

The whole Delaware valley was peopled by the Lenâpé and their sub-tribes, and the country from the Susquehanna to the sea was claimed by them. William Penn, in letters forwarded to England, describes them a very peaceable nation, and they were in no wise involved in the early Colonial wars. Penn also treated directly with the Unami and Un-alachtigo sub-tribes for the land in the first Indian deed dated in the year 1682. The balance of the lands was acquired from the Minsi and Iroquois tribes, who held undisputed possession of a large tract.

The Unami territory also extended to the mouth of the North river, and it was by this means that an offshoot of the tribe, the Mahicanni, settled on the Upper Hudson, taking the same totems, the wolf, the turtle and the turkey. Through some reason they became absorbed in the New England tribes, and lost to a great degree their original tongue.

The Lenâpé name for the strip of land lying between the Delaware river and the Atlantic ocean was Sha-akbee, meaning "long land between water." So, also, they called the river Lenâpé Wihittuck (the stream of the Lenâpé). The name, however, applied only from the ocean to the Forks at Easton. At this point we find the original East and West Branches, the former known as the Lecha, now the Lehigh river. From Easton to Hardenburg Patent, in New York State, the Indian name was Namæ Sipu, or Seepu, (Fish river). The Dutch called it Viskill. As the river became better known through boating and rafting the present name was applied to it from the junction of the Mohawk and Popacton branches, below Hancock, New York, to the Delaware river. The former takes its name from the tribe of the Lenâpé Confederacy.

The Lenni Lenâpé sub-tribes and their location were as follows: The Minsi, or Mountain tribe, with the wolf as the totemic animal, inhabited the country above the Forks of the Delaware. They had two council fires, one at Water Gap and the other on Minisink plains. Their lands extended from the Hudson to and beyond the Susquehanna. The Unami—from the Indian Naheu, meaning down stream— or Turtle tribe, trace their wigwams from the Lehigh valley to the falls at Trenton. The Unalachtigo, or Turkey tribe, designating "the people who live near the ocean," occupied the land from Philadelphia to Wilmington. The low lands about Trenton were settled upon by the Assanhicans, "The Stone-implement People," a small sub tribe, whose lands also extended along the upper Indian path to New York bay.

The legends, traditions and literature of this nation have been well preserved through their prominence in connection with the English proprietaries. The Lenâpé were well versed in the art of pottery-making, copper-smelting and paint-mixing, and relics of their handicraft are constantly found by scientists in the Delaware valley. At Park Island, the retreat of the Trenton canoeists, several fine specimens of arrowheads, stone hatchets and pottery have been unearthed.

A few members of this once powerful and important tribe still exists among the Indians of the far West. Francis Parkman, in his book *The Oregon Trail*, has the following to say: "This tribe, the Delawares, once the peaceful allies of William Penn, the tributaries of the conquering Iroquois, are now (1847) the most adventurous and dreaded warriors upon the prairies. They make war upon remote tribes, the very names of which were unknown to their fathers in the ancient seats in Pennsylvania, and they push these new quarrels with true Indian rancor, sending out their war parties as far as the Rocky mountains, and into the Mexican territories. But the Delawares dwindle every year, from the number of men lost in their war-like expeditions."

One thing is certain: their disappearance from the land of their council fires was remarkably complete. As early as the year 1700 their deterioration commenced, and the last remnant migrated to Ohio in the year 1800. Fifty years later their bands were scattered over the plains beyond the Platte.

To the white man's war-like teachings and the scourges of the day—whiskey and small-pox—can be traced their overthrow. In view of what they once were, their friendliness and readiness to part peaceably with valuable grants, they deserved a better fate.

For, as Milton says—

> "Thus was this place
> A happy rural seat of various views."

APPENDIX 2.

DISTANCES ON THE DELAWARE.

These distances are in the main correct—

Hancock to Stockport Station,   4 1/2 miles.
Stockport to Lordville,   5 3/4 "
Lordville to Long Eddy,   6 3/4 "
Long Eddy to Callicoon,   1 "
Callicoon to Cochecton,   5 1/4 "
Cochecton to Narrowsburg,   8 1/2 "
Narrowsburg to Masthope,   5 3/4 "
Masthope to Westcolang Park,   3 "
Westcolang Park to Lackawaxen,   2 1/2 "
Lackawaxen to Shohola,   4 "
Shohola to Pond Eddy,   8 "
Pond Eddy to Port Jervis,   10 3/4 "
Port Jervis to New Jersey State Line,   2 1/2 "

Total 68 1/4 miles (direct line measurements), passing Equmink, Little Equmink, below Stockport and Lordville; Hankins, below Long Eddy; Parker's Glen, below Shohola; and Matamoras, opposite Port Jervis.

New Jersey State Line to Milford, Pennsylvania,   5 1/4 miles.
Milford to Montague,   3/4 "
Montague to Dingman's Ferry,   6 3/4 "
Dingman's to Bevans, or Peter's Valley,   1 1/2 "

Bevans to Walpack Center,   3 miles
Walpack Center to Bushkill,   6 "
Length of Walpack Bend,   6 "
Bushkill to Millbrook (traveling through Walpack Bend),
2 1/2 "
Millbrook to Calno, 1 1/2 "
Calno to Brotzmansville, 6 "
Brotzmansville to Mouth of Cherry Creek (Water Gap),
1 1/2 "
Cherry Creek to Portland,   5 1/4 "
Portland to Delaware Station,   1 1/2 "
Delaware Station to Ramsaysburg,   1 1/2 "
Ramsaysburg to Manunka Chunk,   1 "
Manunka Chunk to Belvidere (Pequest Creek),   3 3/4 "
Belvidere to Martin's Creek,   6 "
Martin's Creek to Brainard's,   1 1/2 "
Brainard's to Phillipsburg,   5 "
Phillipsburg to Carpenterville (Raubville),   4 1/2 "
Carpenterville to Reigelsville,   2 1/4 "
Reigelsville to Durham Furnace,   2 1/4 "
Durham Furnace to Milford, New Jersey, 5 1/4 "
Milford to Frenchtown,   3 "
Frenchtown to Erwinna,   1 1/2 "
Erwinna to Tumble,   1 1/2 "
Tumble to Lumberville (Raven Rock),   5 1/4 "
Lumberville to Lambertville (Cat Hill),   5 1/4 "
Lambertville to Moore's,   5 "
Moore's to Washington's Crossing,   3 "
Washington's Crossing to Yardley,   4 "
Yardley to Trenton,   4 "

Total distance from New Jersey State line to Trenton,
in a straight line, 109 1/2 miles.

DOWN THE DELAWARE RIVER
IN A CANOE.

Introduction.[*]

This book is not intended as a mere manual for the special use of skilled professional or amateur athletes, though necessarily many of its details refer particularly to these classes. Its main purpose is to bring into consideration the high value, moral and intellectual as well as physical, of those exercises that develop healthy constitutions, cheerful minds, manly self-confidence, and appreciation of the beauties of nature and natural enjoyment. Nevertheless, these lines of Bunyan tell my preliminary experience;—

> "Some said, John, print it; others said, Not so;
> Some said. It might do good; others said, No."

So long as large numbers of our young people, of both sexes, are narrow-chested, thin-limbed, their muscles growing soft as their fat grows hard, timid in the face of danger, and ignorant of the great and varied exercises that are as needful to the strong body as letters to the informed mind, such books as this need no excuse for their publication.

---

[*] These opening paragraphs are excerpted from the introduction to John Boyle O'Reilly's *Athletics and Manly Sport* (Boston, 1890), which contains the essay "Down the Delaware River in a Canoe."

DOWN THE DELAWARE RIVER
IN A CANOE.

"You can run everything on the river but the Big Foul," said the teamster at Port Jervis, as he helped us launch the canoes from a gravel bank.

"Where is the Big Foul?"

"Below Belvidere: you'll strike it in a few days. No boat can run that rift at this stage of the water."

"Oh, it's a rift," said Moseley, standing knee-deep in the river, and packing his canoe. "I thought it was a bird. Why is it called the Big Fowl?"

"It is the foulest rapid on the Delaware," answered the teamster. "I know the river to Trenton: went down last May on a fresh. You can run all the rest; but you'll have to carry round the Big Foul Rift."

We had before heard about this rapid with the ominous name. A discussion in *Forest and Stream*, a few years ago, directed the attention of canoemen to its alleged dangers and extreme rapidity of current.[**]

[**] Two canoemen of East Orange, N. J., who ran the rapids in 1878, and who claimed to be the first to do it, wrote as follows: "After passing through two or three small rifts, we arrived at Great Foul Rift, which is considered the most dangerous one in the river, on account of the number of rocks and the swiftness of the current. How to describe our passage through here, we hardly know; all we can say is, we saw it, we entered it, and we passed it. You can see the big slate rocks on all sides of you, and are unable to tell what min-

I had with me also the notes of one of the best canoe-men in the country, who had run the Delaware in the spring of last year, to which I referred, and found these words:—

> "Great Foul Rift, short distance below Belvidere. Ran down on rafting fresh in May. Length almost a mile and a half from head of Little Foul to foot of Great Foul. Rapidity of water and danger much exaggerated."

"That's all right for a spring fresh," said the teamster,

---

ute you will strike them. This rift is two miles long, and we passed through it in three minutes exactly, being carried that fast by the current, without using our paddles." This statement was received with astonishment. Two miles in three minutes, or forty miles an hour, is not the speed of a rapid, but almost that of a waterfall.

Among the critics was Mr. A. H. Siegfried of Louisville, who had also run the Great Foul Rift. He wrote: "We were warned against Foul Rift for two days above it, and came to it determined not merely to run it, but to examine it carefully, and see if it is as dangerous as the natives think. We went through it without paddle, save for steering purposes, but losing no time from speed of actual current, and were just eleven minutes from the time we entered until we left the swift water. That we thought a quick run, considering the windings of the channel, following which the distance is fully three miles, though a straight line will measure nearly one-third less. The rift is very swift and crooked, whirling among many and such recklessly distributed boulders that the speed claimed by 'F. P. and E. P. D.' would have been sure death to both boats and men if it had been possible."

The official measurements of the Little and Great Foul Rifts are: Little Foul Rift, 768 ft.; Great Foul Rift, 4,620 ft.; distance from head of Little Rift to foot of Great Rift, 1¾ mile. These measurements are probably by the straight line, and not according to the windings of the channel.

who had heard this note read. "But the river is ten feet lower now; and it's the bottom of a river that's dangerous, not the top."

Guiteras was the first in his canoe. "Here goes for Philadelphia!" he cried, as he pushed off.

"Are there any rapids near us, down the river?"

"Listen!" and the teamster smiled.

We listened and heard one, the sound coming from the bend of the river half a mile below.

"It's only a little one," shouted the teamster, as we started. "Keep well to the left, and you'll find a channel. It is a smooth rift."

We were three, in three canoes,—Mr. Edward A. Moseley in a stout boat built by Partelow, of the Charles River; Dr. Ramon Guiteras, in a strong Racine; while mine was a keelless, decked canoe, by the best builder in the world, Rushton, of Canton, N. Y.

It was two in the afternoon of a glorious day when we started from Port Jervis. After a long, dusty railroad ride, it is impossible to convey the exhilarating sense of freedom and enjoyment which one feels during the first moments in his canoe. To plunge the bare arms to the elbow into the river as you go, and let the cool water curl up to the biceps; to feel the soft breeze on bare head and neck; to be far from the busy crowds in the cities, with all the senses awake to new and fascinating objects—the swirl of rapid water, the brown and yellow stones on the bottom of the river, the large, free movements of clouds, the strange flowers on the bank; to grip the paddle with an agreeable sense of power in shoulder and hand; to brace the feet strongly against the foot-rest and feel the canoe spring with the elastic force of the stroke; to shout unrestrainedly to your companions, and hear them shout in return like hearty, natural men; to laugh consumedly with slight cause; and in the midst of all this joyous wakefulness, to be aware of the nearing rapid ahead—to hear its low, steady roar, as if the sound clung to the water; and to be aware also of a new preparation of nerve, sight, and muscle—a purely animal and instinctive alertness—for the moment of rushing excitement into which you are sweeping,—all this we experienced within ten minutes of leaving; the gravel bed at Port Jervis, and while the teamster still shouted to us from the shore.

We were silent at first, and surprised. It took us some moments to realize that the surprise was delight. The river was not deep—three or four feet at most; but it ran down hill like a hunted hare. There was something quite new in it, too, which I concluded to be the long, wavy green weeds near the bottom, that floated straight with the current like a yacht's pennant in a gale, and by their swaying and glistening in the depths indicated the course and the extraordinary rapidity of the water.

"This is superb!" said one. The others echoed the word.

Almost before we knew, we were in the rush of the first rapid. We had not carefully followed the teamster's instructions to keep to the extreme left; and we had passed the narrow mouth of the channel. Before us ran an oblique bar of heavy stones, over which the river poured like a curtain. It ran clear across the river, and we found ourselves far into the closed angle. The water on the curtain to the left roared like a heavy surf, and we knew that we could not get over or through. There was no opening between the stones more than two feet wide, and beyond or below was a hundred yards of chaotic rock and roar.

We turned and paddled up stream—I might have said up hill. Inch by inch we gained, working with feverish speed, the paddle slipping back in the glancing stream as if it were in air, holding hardly any force.

But we climbed the first descent, and steered across to where the channel hugged the right bank. Guiteras went in first; he had not gone up far enough by a boat's length, and as he shot across into the narrow channel, his canoe lurched upon one side, stood a moment and swung athwart stream. He had struck; but before a thought of danger could follow, the paddle was buried, and with a lifting push, his boat slipped over the stone and rushed down the rapid like a leaf.

The other canoes followed, avoiding the buried stone. It was a vigorous little rush—about two hundred yards in length, and not fifteen feet in width. The water was deep, but its speed made it rise in a leap over every stone on the bottom, and hurl itself in all kinds of ridges and furrows and springing white-caps.

At the bottom of the rift we plunged into a heap of boiling breakers, still running like mad. Next moment we floated into smooth water, and turned and looked back at our first rapid with much laughing and congratulation.

The rapid, or rift (on the Upper Delaware all rapids are *rifts*; on the Lower Delaware all rifts are *falls*; the change beginning, I think, about Easton, as, for instance. Saw-mill Rift, Death's Eddy Rift, Big Foul Rift; and below, Welles's Falls, Trenton Falls, etc.)—the rapid we had passed, on looking back, seemed insignificant in descent and roughness; but we were fairly astonished at the speed of the water, and I think we had a vague consciousness that it would have been no child's play to steer through that channel had it been of any considerable length, and broken by rocks. The teamster had called it "a little one," and "a smooth rift"; what, then, were the big ones? There was no mention at all of this rift in the notes of the canoeman which I had with me. What was the ominous Great Foul Rift in comparison?

As we gazed back at the rapid, it receded from us swiftly. We were on the quiet surface of deep water, but going down at the rate of several miles an hour.

The current still kept to the left bank, and an odd bank it was,—worth describing, because it continued intermittently quite down to Trenton where the last rapid on the Delaware pitches the canoeman into tidal water. The bank resembled molten metal that had hardened. It was almost black, a clean, smooth stone, with round puff-holes in it, no vegetation whatever on the steep slope of, say, twenty feet from the water's edge, above which rose a wooded hill, almost a mountain. The metallic bank ended abruptly in the stream, and the deep current alongside ran with astonishing swiftness.

I realized in brief time that up to that day I had not known rapid water, continued in a long stream. The Susquehanna rapids are short and sharp descents, followed by slow and gentle reaches, some of which are miles in length. The Connecticut, in a memory of six years' distance, spreads out like a lake, with here and there a log moving alongshore, showing that there actually is a current. The Merrimack was remembered as a very millpond, except on the short descent of Miller's Falls, near Haverhill, and in the powerful tidal rush under Deer Island Chain-bridge at Newburyport; while many lesser streams were quite forgotten in presence of this grand artery which carried us onward almost as fast as we could paddle on slower rivers.

I have given too much space to our first rapid on the Delaware, which, we soon found, was only one of scores before us, and a small one—even a "smooth one." But it will save other descriptions; and it gives our first impression of the river. Having run the Delaware from Port Jervis to Philadelphia, we found that this first rapid was singularly characteristic. All the considerable rapids are of a somewhat similar formation,—except the Great Foul Rift, which is unique.

The rapids of the Delaware are formed in the main by an oblique line of rocks crossing the river, leaving a narrow channel on one side, or sometimes the opening is almost one-third of the way across, with reefs on both sides.

With deep water, say in May or June, when the river is from eight to ten feet higher than it was in the last week of August, a canoeman may run two hundred miles of this incomparable river without striking a stone. But every foot of fall in the stream makes a totally new river; and he who goes down on a freshet in early summer cannot imagine what the river is like at low water in late autumn.

The Delaware is a river of extraordinary pitch, the fall from Port Jervis to Philadelphia being nearly 1,200 feet.

On that first afternoon we intended to run down to Milford, twelve miles distant, where, we had been told, there was a famous hotel. But we lingered on the way. In the sweltering heat we pulled the canoes ashore and plunged into the delicious water, drinking it as we swam—a sensation for epicures. We lay prone in the rapid stream, our arms outspread, and our faces under water, floating quickly down, and looking at the yellow and white pebbles on the bottom.

At last we came to a lovely spot, a soft white sand-bank on the left, the Jersey side, formed by the junction of a bright little river with the Delaware. Every paddle was laid down. Half a mile below we heard the dull roar of a rapid. Here the river was very deep and swift, and not more than eighty yards wide. On the right, a wooded but precipitous mountain rose almost straight from the water to a height of at least 800 feet. From his eyrie far up we had disturbed a white-headed eagle which floated and tipped its great wings above us as it moved slowly down river.

The sand-bank was in the angle where the little river fell over a short rapid of twenty yards into the Delaware. The bank was hemmed in by a dense wood.

"We camped on the sand-bank for the night. One man erected the tent; another cooked dinner; the third went in search of a farmhouse for milk, eggs, melons and peaches—the staple of our food for the next fortnight.

While the dinner simmered we had a trial of strength with the Delaware itself, breast to breast. Swiftly we struck across and down the river for a hundred yards, and then turned and faced the stream. Three strong swimmers,—two of the three extraordinary. Moseley, with the over-hand stroke, which sends him about eight feet a stroke in still water, made progress at the rate of about one foot a stroke. Guiteras barely held his own, swimming as if he were anchored; and, watching the bank, I saw that I was actually going down stream. Under such circumstances you can do a great deal of swimming in a quarter of an hour.

The sun went down on the left, above the low trees, without cloud or haze. For a long time after its disappearance the upward rays flamed on the face of the great cliff across the river, the red gleam moving higher and higher, and the darkness creeping up the wooded wall like a vast tide. When the line of light had cleared the brow of the cliff the trees above, diminished to a finger-length, blazed in gold and crimson: and then, almost suddenly, the light left them,—rose over them, and was lost in space, and they, too, were swallowed up in the night.

"The light that shoots over the heads of trees or people," said Moseley, "might as well not exist."

With which philosophic reflection, we spread our rubber blankets on the sand of the tent, over these our woolen blankets; and then, with a big fire blazing a few feet from the tent's mouth, we lay or sat for our coffee and cigars.

Throughout our trip this quiet smoking hour, each evening with a strange scene before us, was a most enjoyable part of the day.

We slept as if the night were an hour long, and we woke to plunge into the sweet unchilled water. We started without breakfast, hoping to reach Milford and the "famous cook" at an early hour.

The miles were long, and the river unendingly broken. It was down hill all the time, rift succeeding rift. Do what we could with careful steering, we struck again and again, and we were in constant danger of smashing boats or paddles. So common became the striking that we coined a word for it—"hung up." And we could not help laughing, when one struck, as we swept past and saw him grimly poling his canoe over a rock, or raising his feet over the gunwale, as he got out to haul her over. For this we had to be always ready; trousers tucked up, and canvas shoes on.

It came to be a jesting habit, that when one led into a rapid he would do so with a boastful shout. This was my part, at one time on this second day. I had gone into a rift with much flourish, and, a third of the way through, had been "hung up." Down rushed the others with loud derision, avoiding the bad place. Imagine my feelings of disgust at their selfishness, as I saw their backs, leaving me there. Next moment, in the worst part of the rapid, I saw one of them strike and hold his boat with his paddle against a rock; and a second or two later the other struck just beside him. Who could help smiling? And that moment, by a fortunate lurch, my canoe floated and rushed down toward the two, who were now struggling knee-deep in the stream. They held on to let me pass, and scowled as if my laugh were in bad taste.

At ten o'clock we reached Milford, Penn., and climbed the hundred feet of steep bank on which the little town stands. Over the town, all round, rose still many hundred feet of grandly-wooded mountains. The hotel, they told us, was over twelve hundred feet above sea level. The hotel we found to be even better than its report.

Ever since starting at Port Jervis, Moseley had kept referring to the beauty of the scenery at Walpack Bend, some fifteen or twenty miles below Milford. He had a camera with him, and his desire to get out and take a view grew on him like a disease. No impatience, or protest, or prayer affected him. "When we get home," he would unselfishly say, "these pictures will be the best part of the trip,"—and he was right.

The banks on both sides now rose into mountains, wooded to the top. The river was a series of deep and swift reaches, and then a leaping rift, with a steep descent.

In the very centre of one of these rapids, an unusually deep one, my canoe struck on a covered rock and I knew in a flash that she must either get instantly over or be rolled down stream. Thought and act united. I lifted her by a vigorous push, and was whirled down, stern foremost, with my paddle broken.

Fortunately, the channel below was deep, though rough and very rapid. To meet the emergency I knelt up, instead of sitting as heretofore, and used the broken end of the paddle as a pole, fending off rocks, and steering occasionally with the blade end.

Before I had cleared the rapid I knew that my loss was a gain. The best way to steer a canoe down a rapid is to kneel and use *a long paddle with one blade, the other end to he used as a pole.*

I had a spare paddle in the canoe, a delicate spoon paddle, only fit for deep water. As soon as the rift was past, I jointed this and used it; but when the next rift was heard, laid it aside and took up the broken paddle.

The memory of that day is wholly confused with the noise of rapid water. We were no sooner through one rift than we heard another. The names of the rapids were quaint and suggestive: such as Death's Eddy, Fiddler's Elbow, Milliner's Shoe, Sambo and Mary, Vancamp's Nose, and Shoemaker's Eddy.

One must use colors, not words, to paint the beauty of the scene that opened before us on our third day, when we ran the upper rapid at Walpack Bend, and floated into a reach of river that can hardly be surpassed in the world. On our right and left the banks were low and richly timbered; and straight ahead, barring our way, about half a mile off, a high mountain, wooded from the water to the crest.

The river runs straight to the mountain-foot, and there turns directly to the left. It is not a curve or a sweep, but distinctly a right angle; and then, for one mile with the hill to the right and the low farms on the left, and for two miles with the mountain to the left and the farms to the right, the grand stream paces slowly, like a proud horse in the eye of a multitude.

Here we had a striking illustration of the power of color. The wooded height before us rose at least twelve hundred feet. The river below was green with the immense reflection. But on the very line of union, where the leaves met and kissed in air and water, was a little flame of crimson, which held the eye and centered all the immensity.

It was one small cardinal flower, a plant that grows all the way along the Delaware. The intensity of its color is indescribable. After this superb exhibition of its power, one little red flower against a mile of green and silver, I gathered every day a handful of the lovely blossoms and set them on the bow of the canoe.

When one thinks of the marvels of this river, the regret becomes painful that they are unknown to the outer world, that they are only seen by the natives of the scenes and the accidental canoe voyager.

The rivers are the veins and arteries of a country, the railroads and roads the nerves and sinews.

He has seen the land truly, with its wealth and strength, who has followed the rivers from their sources in the hills down to the tide-pulsating ocean-heart. But the railroads are familiar, the rivers unknown. "Sin writes histories," says Goethe; "goodness is silent."

The river affects men in a different way from the road. The dweller by the railroad is keen and quick to trade, and dicker, and undertake. The inhabitants of the river valleys are placid folk; farmers content with their peaceful and laborious lives.

Such homes as the poets have imagined are realities on every mile of the Delaware's banks. Never before, in the same space, have I seen so many quiet, contented, and gentle working people. Scores and hundreds of farmhouses we passed, surrounded with flowers and foliage, the easy-chairs waiting on the wide porch, with the women sitting sewing, the children playing near the house, the men working in the farmyard or in the spreading melon or peach fields, and the bright river moving forever before their eyes, with its great homely ferry-boat waiting below, where the shaded paths comes down the bank. Softly come to one's memory the lines of Bryant,

"O River, gentle River! gliding on
In silence underneath this cloud-flecked sky
Thine is a ministry that never rests,
Even while the living slumber.

At dead of night the child awakes and hears
Thy soft, familiar dashings, and is soothed,
And sleeps again."

But one is tempted to linger too long on such a scene as this at Walpack Bend. Here, for the first time since we left Port Jervis, the water ran slowly. It is hard to leave a spot so beautiful, where so few strangers are led. Here was Nature at first hand. To impress it deeper on my mind, I retrace our course, on the bank, to where, a hundred yards above the bend, a little singing river flows into the Delaware. Only a few inches deep, babbling over brown pebbles, bright as the sun itself in its flashes, coming down under a dim arch of trees and fringing underwood—a very dream of a little singing brook, that

"Knows the way to the sea."

Here, sitting on a stone, enjoying the soft susurrus in my ears and in the leaves and in the ripples, comes along a country boy, fishing—down the dim arch, walking in the little river, barefooted.

"Bushmill Creek is its name," he says; and he knows no more about it—not how long it is, nor whence it comes.

But yet a commentator and critic, this barefooted fisher.

"How far have you fellows come?" he asked, examining the canoes.

"From Port Jervis."

"And how far are you going?"

"To Philadelphia."

"Well,"—a long pause—"you fellows must want something to do!"

A song sung by some country girls and boys in a boat, passing close to the mountain foot, makes a memory of music and echo as vivid as the gleam of the cardinal flower. They slowly move their unwieldly-looking crooked oars, characteristic of the Delaware—the flat blade set on the oar at an obtuse angle. But this oar, hinged on the gunwale of the flat-bottomed boat, or bateau, is suited to a river of rifts, the bent blade enabling the rower to sweep the shallow water without striking.

The river is rich with bass, and the fishers are numerous. Below Walpack Bend, a lady in a boat, excited and joyous, holds up a splendid fish as we pass.

"See! I've just caught it!" she says. It was at least five pounds weight. A gentleman in the boat tells us that we can run all the rapids down the river—"except the Great Foul Rift!"

Here it was again; and from this time forward, almost every one to whom we spoke warned us in about the same words. Hence grew an unexpressed desire in each of our minds to get away from this croaking rapid; we longed to reach and run it, and have done with it.

But we were approaching one of the glories of the Delaware—the most famous and certainly the most sublime—the Water Gap. We reached it unexpectedly. We knew when it was only a few miles away, but we could see nothing ahead but the unbroken mountain range on each side. One mile away, and the range had closed around us in a bight, leaving no perceptible opening for the river.

"Where is the Water Gap?" we asked a boatful of fishers, anchored under a bridge.

"You'll see it in half a minute," they answered. "And look out! for just round the turn there, you will be in the rapid."

We did not need the warning; we were in the quick water already. Looking into the stream, we saw the yellow stones on the bottom fly sternward at an extraordinary pace. The roar of a powerful rapid reached us as we came to a sharp turn in the river; and below us we saw a memorable scene.

I do not know the descending angle of that rapid, nor the measure of its fall; but it seemed as if we were on the top of a hill of rushing water, at the bottom of which, less than a mile away, was a vast wooded basin, its green slope broken by two white hotels set on the hillside, but still seemingly far below us.

There was no time for admiration, or for anything but steering. We ran down the Jersey shore, close to the rocky mountain foot, in the fastest rush so far. The river plunged from ledge to ledge fiercely; but the channel was deep. At the foot of the fall, we were shot into a whirlpool of yellow breakers that curled up and washed clean over the canoes, drenching all, and almost swamping one of them.

We stopped at the Water Gap that night, and sat long on the wide veranda of the hotel, looking at the wonderful scene. The river passes between two mountains, as through a tremendous gateway; and one feels, without knowing, that beyond that imperial portal, the scene must change into something quite new and strange.

This we found to be true: the Delaware may be said to have left the mountains when it pours through the Water Gap. Henceforth, its banks are bold, or even precipitous, as the right bank surely is in a wonderful cliff some miles below Reigelsville; but it is a mountain river no longer.

In the morning, before starting, we climbed the mountain and looked down on the wild beauty of the Water Gap. From that height the fall in the river was imperceptible; and the rapid that had astonished us the day before looked like a mere shallow brawl.

Few people are aware of the force and danger of rapid broken water. To the person who drives or walks along a river, the rapid seems the safest spot, because it is obviously the shallowest. But, as the teamster said at Port Jervis, it is "the bottom that is to be feared, not the top."

"It is just the same with humanity," says Guiteras, when this thought is spoken; "it is the superficial and hasty people who make all the trouble. Depth of mind is as safe as depth of water."

The last word to us from the boat-keeper at the Water Gap was, of course, a warning about the Great Foul Rift. We ran two or three rapids that day that tested nerves and boats, and were exasperated to hear that they were "smooth rifts," and "nothing at all to the Big Foul."

In the high heat of the afternoon, we came to a place where a little waterfall leaped down a bank almost twenty feet into the river. The falling water was white as snow. We went under it and enjoyed a glorious shower bath, but found that in the centre the water fell in lumps almost as heavy and hurtful as clay.

That day, too, we had another novel and delightful experience. We came to an unbroken reach of river on which the descent was so great that a stretch of two miles before us resembled a coasting-hill of ice. The river was about five feet deep, with a gravel bottom. We let the canoes float, and we followed, with outspread arms and faces in the water, fairly coasting down that wonderful liquid slope.

Late in the evening, not finding a pleasant camping place, we settled at last on a tolerable spot, on an island. We were tired, and we soon fell asleep—to be awakened by a shout of horror from Guiteras, over whose hand a snake had crawled! He had flung the reptile from him, out of the tent.

After such a start, sleep was out of the question. We lay, however, and tried to rest. But every rustle of the leaves outside, every insect that stirred in the grass, brought a chill and creepy feeling.

"I am going to sleep in the canoe," at last said one; and at the word we gathered our blankets and abandoned the tent.

If it were not for the danger of straining the boat if pulled ashore, or of catching malaria if it be left afloat, the canoe is the pleasantest and easiest sleeping place.

In the morning a swim, a solid breakfast, and an extra careful packing of the canoes. No one spoke of it; but that morning we were each conscious of a particular attention paid to the trim of the boats and the stowing of dunnage. At about eleven o'clock in the forenoon we would reach Belvidere; and the Great Foul Rift was only a mile farther.

There was a camp of bass fishers near us, and they came to see us start. They learned our intention of going down without portage, rift or no rift. They did not dissuade us. One of them said he knew the Big Foul Rift, and he gave us precise, too precise, instructions. All I could recall half an hour later was: "Keep to the right when you come to the big white stone—if there's water enough to float your boats."

It was noon when we came to the town of Belvidere, and paddled into deep water under a mill. We needed some necessaries for our dinner, and we could buy them here. The school-boys flocked to the bank to see the canoes, and the mill-workers (it was the dinner hour) came down to have a chat.

"You are not going to run the rift?" asked one.

"Yes, we are."

"They can do it: they don't draw more than two inches," said another.

We knew that at least one of the canoes, heavily laden with baggage, and with a heavy man in her, drew more than six inches. We could get no information worth having, except a repetition of the fisherman's word: "Keep to the right of the big rock, two-thirds of the way down,—if you can."

"Nobody has gone down the rift for five weeks," said the man who had first spoken.

Guiteras was going ashore for the necessaries; and as he stood in his canoe, about to step on a log that edged the bank, he slipped, and pitched head-first into the deep water. We were so used to going into the water anyway, that the other two sat quite still in the canoes, as if not heeding, while Guiteras climbed out and shook himself, in a matter-of-course kind of way. This nonchalance created an impression on the crowd; and shortly after, when we started, the general prediction was audibly in our favor.

"Keep to the right of the big white rock, and you will strike the channel," shouted a man as we started.

Half a mile or so below Belvidere, we felt the water quicken and sweep to the right—the Pennsylvania bank. We knew we were in the first reach of the rapid that had been roaring for us since we started.

There are two distinct rapids,—the Little Foul and the Great Foul,—divided by a reach of safe but swift water of half a mile.

From the moment we struck the Little Foul Rift, we knew we were in the grip of a giant. We were as much astonished as if we had never run a rapid before. We shot down the river—each one finding his own channel—like chips; and, with all our careful steering, we grazed several dangerous stones.

There was no stopping at the foot of the Little Foul Rift; but we ran with the stream without paddling, and examined the entrance to the Great Rapid ahead.

There was no bar or ledge formation here, as in the minor rifts behind us. The rocks stood up like the broken teeth of a sperm whale, irregularly across the river, and as far ahead as we could see from the canoes. Some of the stones were twelve feet out of the water, others of lesser height, and of all shapes; some were level with the surface, and some covered with a few inches of water. These last were the dangers: to strike and get "hung up" on one of these meant certain upsetting: for no boat could stand the rush, and there was no footing for the canoeman if he tried to get out to push her over.

But more threatening than the tall rocks, that looked like a disorganized Stonehenge, was the terrible nature of the bed rock, and the broken stones on the bottom. We could steer between the teeth we saw, but we suddenly became conscious of unseen teeth that lay in wait to lacerate the boats under the water-line.

The whole bed of the river is formed of a rock that is worn and wasted in a strangely horrible way, as if it were pitted with a hideous smallpox. Round and oval holes are seen everywhere in the rock, some of them as much as two feet deep and three feet across; and the upper edges of these bowls are as sharp as scythes.

We saw the process of this singular pitting. Heavy stones are caught on an angle of the bottom and rolled over and over without proceeding, till they wear out these cup-like holes, and are buried deeper and deeper in their ceaseless industry. As the bowl increases in size, it catches two workers instead of one, and these grind each other and grind the matrix till the very heart of Nature must admit their toil, and pity their restlessness.

Some of these great stone cups were high out of water, empty and dry; and their round tormentors lay in peace on the bottom. Some were above the surface, but still half full of water that had dashed into them from the rapid.

But there was a keener evil than the circular knife tops of these vessels; and it was their broken edges.

When the torrents of winter and spring thunder through the Great Foul Rift, whirling and dragging trunks of trees and massive stones down the surcharged channels, the pitted ledges of bottom and bank are smashed like potsherds, the imprisoned stones are released and shoot down the river, and the fractured rock remains to cut the water with irregular edges as sharp as a shattered punch-bowl.

We were going into the Great Foul Rift all this time, at the rate of—but who can tell the rate of rapid water? The best canoeman I know says there is no canoeing-water in America over twelve miles an hour,—I think he places this on the Susquehanna, below Columbia,—and that eight miles is very rapid indeed. He may be right; but, were I asked how fast we went into the Great Foul Rift, I should say, at least, at the rate of twelve miles an hour, and, in parts of the descent, much faster.

Guiteras went first, but was caught on a covered flat stone in the quick, smooth water; and Moseley led into the rapid, Guiteras, who had floated off, following. I came about fifty yards behind.

From the first break of the water, the sensation was somewhat similar to that of falling through the branches of a tree. The river was twisting down-hill in convulsions. We rushed through narrow slopes of ten or twenty feet as if we were falling; and then shot round a rock, flinging the whole weight of our bodies on the steering-paddle. The tall stones ahead seemed to be rushing at us with the velocity of an ocean steamer.

All the time we were painfully conscious of the presence of the incisive edges under water, as one might feel the nearness of burglars' knives in the night. If we struck one of these stones on a downward shoot, it would rip the canoe from bow to stern.

Moseley steered skilfully, and we cleared two-thirds of the tortuous descent without a shock. A quarter of a mile ahead we saw the smooth water at the foot of the rift. We had crossed the river, and were running down on the Pennsylvania shore. Suddenly, the channel we were in divided at a great white stone, the wider water going to the left, toward the centre of the river, and a narrow black streak keeping straight down to the right.

A memory of the warning came to me, "Keep to the right of the big rock,—if you can." But it was too late. A man could not hear his own shout in such an uproar. The white rock rushed past us. The canoes ahead had turned with the main stream, and were in the centre of the river in a flash. Suddenly both canoes ahead were shot out of the channel, their bows in the air resting on a hidden rock; and the current, just then turning a sharp curve, swept by their sterns with a rush. Fortunately they were out of the stream, driven into an eddy, or that had been the end of them.

I had time to profit by their mishap. Kneeling in the canoe, using the long-handled paddle, I rounded the curve within a foot of the grounded canoes, and fairly leaped downhill on a rounded muscle of water. In the rush, a thrill swept my nerves—and another—as if twice I had touched cold steel. I found later that my canoe had twice been pierced by the knife-like edges under water.

Before I realized it, the end had come, and the canoe shot across the river in a sweeping eddy. The Great Foul Rift was behind me.

A fisherman on the bank had been watching our passage. "You ought to have kept to the right of that stone," he shouted. "See, there's the channel!" And, looking up, I saw it, straight as a furrow from the big white stone, keeping swift, close to the Pennsylvania shore, unbroken, and safe. Had we kept in this straight way the Great Foul Rift would to us have been no more than an exaggerated name.

The grounded canoemen pushed free, and were down in a minute; and then we went ashore, and while Moseley photographed the Great Foul Rift, the others plunged into the delicious water, that seemed too peaceful and sweet ever to have been violent and brutal.

Half a mile below the Great Foul Rift, we came to the pastoral scene of the voyage, *par excellence*. It was ideal and idyllic—sunny and varied as a Watteau painting. It was not great or grand in any way; but simply peaceful, pastoral, lovely.

It was a sloping hillside, of two or three farms, rising from the river. There were low-roofed homesteads, smothered in soft domestic-looking foliage. A round-arched stone bridge spanned a stream in the foreground. Cows and horses stood in the shadow of the trees in the fields, and a drove of cows stood in the river, the reflection as distinct as the cow—like Herrick's swans, that "floated double—swan and shadow." Dark woods framed the scene on both sides and on top, children's voices at play filled the air, and a dog barked joyously, joining in some romping game.

We laid our paddles on the canoes in front of us, and floated a full mile through the lovely picture. It can never be forgotten. In its quiet way, nothing equaled it on the whole river.

"Photograph the place," I said to Moseley.

"No," he replied. "It is too good for any thing but memory."

And then followed a rare picture of another kind, or rather a piece of statuary. We had stopped to cook and eat a noble bass, We sat on the bank, near a coscy farm-house, which nestled in trees a little withdrawn from the river. The farmer, a young, roughly-clad man, with laughing bright eyes and a brown, good-humored face, came down the shady road, riding a great draught-horse, and leading another. Following him, were his two little sons, perhaps ten and twelve years old.

He chatted pleasantly with us, while he unlaced his heavy boots, and undressed.

"Are you going to swim?" asked Guiteras.

"I am going to wash my horses," he said.

Just then he pulled his gray woolen shirt over his head, and stood naked beside the horse, preparing to jump on his back. We fairly shouted with admiration, the man was so superbly handsome, and so marvelously muscular. He smiled pleasantly, as if not surprised, jumped on his horse and rode into the deep water; his two yellow-haired boys sitting on the bank, with their hands clasped in front of their legs, watching their father with profound pleasure.

We were accustomed to seeing athletes in training; but none of us had ever seen the equal of this man. He swam his horses out in the deep water for a quarter of an hour, riding like a Centaur, every muscle on his lithe body sinking, gathering, contracting, disappearing, in the most astonishing way. He was not a tall or heavy man. When dressed, he was almost common looking. But never a Greek or Roman gladiator, in life or marble, was more beautiful or more powerful than that young Jersey farmer.

When we came to float the canoes, after dinner, I saw, with dismay, that mine was almost half full of water. In a glance, I realized the meaning of the quick tremors that had chilled me in the last rush of the Great Foul Rift. The canoe had been struck twice under the water-line by the keen-edged rocks.

I feared that the end of my trip had come; but we emptied the water and found that the leaks, which were clean-cut, as if by a knife, had swelled, and almost closed. Easton was a dozen or fifteen miles away; and when we got there, Moseley thought he could patch the canoe with resin and linen and make her water-tight.

But it was a heavy paddle, though the stream raced downhill. One of the cuts was bruised afresh, in a rapid about four miles above Easton, and the water spurted into the canoe.

It was dark to blackness on a Saturday night as we paddled down to Easton. We had been told of a strong rapid just above the city, but we could not see it; we could only hear it, the roar doubled by the night and the imagination. We had run two or three small rifts in the dusk, and had escaped pretty well; and there was nothing for us but to venture again, in the dark, for nowhere could we find a place to land or leave our canoes.

Heavy as a sick animal, my poor little waterlogged boat wallowed along. To strike now was doubly dangerous, for her weight would smash her, bow or beam. The other canoes went ahead. We had been instructed to keep "on the Jersey side of the island." When we entered the rapids, we only paddled for steerage-way. The men ahead kept shouting to me; but, when the rush of the fall came, I was too far to the right, and I brought up heavily on the very outermost stone of the reef.

The canoe was so firmly fixed, that I could have stayed there all night, by sitting quiet. I tried to push off, but could not. I tried to get out; but the stone was sloping, and offered no footing. The water, visible only for a few feet, like a flood of ink, ran with tremendous force on both sides of the stone. The other canoes were out of hearing; and the night was as black as the inside of a cave, with the bright, electric lights of the city, a quarter of a mile away, set upon what seemed high cliffs above the river.

However it was to be done, I must get out, and ease the canoe off the rock. This was one of the minutes in which the disgusted canoeman resolves to give up the sport. If I pushed her over, down stream, I could never hold her to get in: she must be pulled back, and then pushed round the stone. Slowly and cautiously, I got out, and into the water behind the stone, which was almost waist-deep. When the canoe was pulled back, I got in, with some trouble; and a few minutes later joined the others at the end of the rift.

Then began a hunt for a landing. We found that, in the city of Easton, there is not a single landing-place where we could put up our boats for the night. At last we were directed to a place where boats were kept on the bank, on the Jersey side; and there we found an obliging and interesting man named John Horn (the boys called him "Tippy" Horn), who allowed us to carry the canoes up on his rocks, and who stored our baggage, and then rowed us across to Easton.

He was an old river-man; and he said that he had never seen the water so low as it was then. He was a type of the calm, polite, and intelligent common people we had met everywhere on the Delaware. He spoke so slowly and enunciated his syllables so clearly, with his r's burring strongly, that you listened to his sensible sentences with odd pleasure.

That night we stopped at an excellent hotel in Easton; and, while enjoying the pleasant rest of room and bed instead of tent and sand, we received a visit from two genial canoemen, who were on a pedestrian tour through the mining districts, and who recognized our names on the register. One was Mr. Kirk Monroe, then president of the New York Canoe Club; and the other, Mr. Rogers, the artist, whose clever sketches in *Life* and other periodicals have made his reputation national.

We found the citizens of Easton suffering from the intolerable system of the "Law-and-Order" fanatics, who controlled the town, and who had established a system of secret espionage of which the police were used as the tools.

Next day, on the rocks, assisted by Mr. Horn and Mr. Horn's two or three children, and pleasantly watched by a sitting ring of smoking foundrymen, Moseley heated his resin, and patched the damaged Blanid from stem to stern. We found that the sharp edges of the Great Foul Rift had cut her as a bravo cuts his victim. When we floated her, she had anything but a racing bottom; but she was as tight as a drum.

Below Easton, opposite the great rolling-mill, we saw a sight of striking effect,—a multitude of men and boys—perhaps a hundred altogether stripped for swimming, and standing on the high bank. They were outlined against the sky; and as we passed them a hundred yards off, they seemed models of lightness and grace. It was probably the great number of white bodies that made the scene so strange.

Such peaches as we lived on that day—such cantelopes, such melons! Such an island as we camped on, with clean sand as soft as flour! Such a spring pouring out of the mountain across the river, the water as cold as ice, and as clear as liquid diamonds! We enjoyed it with the keenness born of regret; for next day one of our party would have to leave the river.

At Reigelsville, next day, a little Jersey town on a high bank, Moseley boarded the train with his canoe. The other two proceeded; but it was lonely for a day or two, and we sadly missed the strong canoeman and the cheery companion who had left us.

A few miles below Reigelsville the river makes a dive down hill, without breaking, so that we seemed to be on a level with the tops of trees growing on the bank a mile ahead. At the foot of such a decline, we heard the growl of a rapid, and found a division in the river, formed by an island. We kept to the left: we ought to have kept to the right. With a few touches, I got through; but Guiteras was "hung up" in the worst part of the rapid. He tried all ways to get off without leaving the boat: but he had to come to it in the end. And a dangerous time he had for a few minutes. The water was deep, and the powerful current swept the boat against his body, and nearly upset him. He had hard work to hold her back, and get in without capsizing.

Then we came to one of the noblest features of the whole river. On our right, rising sheer as a wall from the water, was a cliff, which must be several hundred feet high. It was formed of layers of rock, each layer perhaps forty or fifty feet deep, and each differing a little in color from the others, so that it looked like a vast storied building. On the narrow ledge at the foot of each layer, trees and shrubs grew, so that the whole face of the cliff was softened with foliage which was so feathery that still the entire wall was visible. In places it was like the outer barrier of a mighty fortress; and in others there was an absolute likeness to artificial masonry.

This majestic cliff ran for perhaps a mile, and then ended abruptly in a soft green hillside of cultivated fields.

But our last rapid had started the leaks in my canoe, and I was bailing every few hundred yards. As the evening was closing, and it threatened rain, we resolved to carry the canoes into the canal, get aboard a canal-boat, and mend the broken Blanid.

The tow-path was only a hundred yards from the river. A hearty canal-man made us welcome on his boat which had a hundred tons of coal on board. His name, he told us, was "Johnnie Curran, from Bristol, down the river." His mate was a small, foxy man, called " Billy," who spoke and walked like a paralytic; but a civil fellow when he got a little present.

"Johnnie" Curran was about thirty-three years old; rather below middle stature, but strong and active, with a stern face, like a fighting man; but with a merry eye and a smile in keeping, so that his features were lit up with constant good-humor and good-nature. He had lost two front teeth, and there was a deep scar on his forehead.

Everyone knew him on the tow-path and the canal.

He was constantly hailing some friend, man or woman, by familiar names, or returning like friendly salutations. He had been canalling "twenty years, like his father before him." He had never known so poor a year as this for canalmen.

But, poor as he was, he threw a loaf or something else to every poor tramp we passed on the tow-path.

He was called, and he called himself, "Johnnem."

In the night (we slept on his boat, which was tied to the bank) we heard passing hails: "Who are you?" "Johnnem." "Hello, Johnnem; hope you're well!"

A memorable incident occurred while we were on Johnnem's boat. We passed a canalside inn, where men and mules are housed. The landlord, an old canaller, sat at the door, and hailed us warmly.

"Who did you have over Sunday?" asked Johnnie Curran.

"Oh, we had a good time—a lot of the right sort. We had Barrett, and Patterson, and Alleghany—and a lot more; and then—we had Mike!"

"Mike! Well, then, you *did* have a good time. Where was he going?"

"Went down to Lambertville, last night."

"Good by!"

"Good luck, Johnnem!"

Then Johnnie told us what a "good fellow" Mike was, and how popular on the canal. We soon had evidence to that effect. A boat, passing, entertained us with an account of "a great time" with Mike the night before.

Presently we passed a pretty little cottage between the canal and the river; over the low garden gate leant a young woman, whom Johnnie Curran saluted thus:

"Evenin', Julia."

"Evenin', Johnnem."

Johnnie, with a wink at us, to cover his duplicity: "Mike here Sunday?"

"No," sulkily; "but he was up at Steele's."

"Well—he'll come next Sunday."

"Don't care if he never comes."

"Oh, yes you do. Good-by, Julia."

"No, I don't. Good-by Johnnem." Pause of moment. "Say, Johnnem!"

"What is it?"

"You needn't tell Mike I said that."

"No fear, Julia. I'll tell him to come up Sunday."

And Johnnie Curran laughed low to himself, as if he knew the ways of womankind. It was a dismal drizzly evening, and we had to go along till ten o'clock. Then, at Lambertville, we were to tie up till morning. As the night grew the rain increased, and at ten it was a steady downpour. We were grateful for the shelter of the stifling little cabin of the canal-boat, where "Billy" snored, and "Billy's" dog had convulsive dreams, in one of which he plunged over Guiteras, and scratched his face.

It was about five next morning when we started. I was half asleep in the cabin when I heard a man shout from the tow-path.

"Johnnem, did you hear about Mike?"

There was something in the man's tone that made me sit up and listen.

"What about him?"

"He's down there on the lock—drowned!"

"God!" hissed Johnnie Curran, as if he had been struck by a missile. "Drowned, you say?"

"Dead! We took him out of the canal last night. He fell in comin' aboard. Poor Mike!"

When we came to the lock, Johnnie Curran jumped ashore and joined the group of canal-men, who stood near the body. They moved aside to let Johnnie see; and he stood with folded arms a full minute looking down at Mike. Then he drew a long breath, and turned away, rapidly brushing his eyes with his hand, and came aboard. He went on with his work without a word, though it was obvious that the dead man had been an old and close friend.

We crossed the river in Johnnie Curran's boat, and left him soon after, carrying our canoes down to the river. Welles's Falls, at Lambertville, had not water enough to float us through. The run before us was about ten miles to Trenton, and the stream was swift. It was a perfect afternoon, clear, warm, and calm. The scenery above Trenton is surprisingly beautiful, though there is no elevation higher than the tree-tops. It was a superb open picture of river and reflection, wood and cloud, with the city spires in the distance seen under the square openings of two extraordinarily-handsome bridges. It would be difficult to name, in the world, a more beautiful opening to a city than the four miles of the Delaware above Trenton.

"The Trenton Canoe Club" was the legend printed on a boat-house under the shadow of the city bridge; and there we stopped.

The house was closed; but we went up to the genial toll-keeper of the bridge,—a venerable man, with a face like George Washington, and a manner to equal it,—who stored our traps and directed us to the hotel. The old man pointed out the difficulties of Trenton Falls, below the bridge, and said that he had hardly ever seen the water so low.

"I'll go with you myself, to-morrow!" said the courteous veteran; "I'll take a boat and show you the way down the falls."

Next morning he was "as good as his word"; but we had with us the president of the Canoe Club, who ran down the intricate channel of the falls, readily and pleasantly chatting all the while. He was in a light canoe, which he handled splendidly.

"A few years ago, before we began canoeing here," he said, "everyone dreaded these falls. Nobody ever ran them but the lumbermen. Now we come down in our canoes for fun, and drag the boats back alongshore."

At the bottom of the falls, which are more portentous in name and aspect than in descent or velocity, we entered tidal water. No more rapids or rifts to Philadelphia, or the sea. The kindly Trenton canoeman left us with a manly grip that was pleasant to remember; and, with the wind and tide against us, we started for Philadelphia, forty-five miles away.

Below Trenton the Delaware is uninteresting for canoemen. We were so used to swift water that we seemed to be anchored while paddling under adverse circumstances. We stopped at Florence that night, and next day shipped our canoes on a river steamer, and ran down to Philadelphia.

Looking back, we salute the Delaware with love and admiration. It has filled our minds with memories and pictures to be cherished for a life time. Noblest of rivers for canoemen, but only for those who come before the middle of July. In the freshets of May and June, a run down the Delaware must be a revelation of joy. Then, not one rock of all that beset our way would be visible or dangerous. We came down a depleted vein: in early summer the Delaware is a full artery. But with all these drawbacks, on our list of canoeing-rivers we must give the first place to the Delaware.

Colophon

Hunter Blair, Megan Marroquin, Suzanne McConlogue, Victoria Orlowski, Juliana Reyes, and Emily D. Siriano, editing interns at Stockton University, assisted with establishing the text, design, and typesetting of this work.

The body text is 11.5 point Minion Pro. Chapter headings are 11.5 point P22 Franklin Caslon. Tom Kinsella completed the frontispiece map, based on a modified US Geological Survey map; he completed the cover, too.

This is a publication of the South Jersey Culture & History Center. Our mission is to foster awareness within local communities of the rich cultural and historical heritage of southern New Jersey, to promote the study of this heritage, especially among area students, and to produce publishable materials that provide a lasting and deepened understanding of this heritage.

ADDITIONAL NATURE TITLES
PUBLISHED BY SJCHC.

Pineys: The People of the New Jersey Pine Barrens
Yael Aravah

Yael Aravah's beautiful photography and interviews with local residents give readers a glimpse into the world of the Pine Barrens. The work explores the notion of identity beyond stereotypes and stigma, asking Pine Barrens residents whether they consider themselves Pineys and what being a Piney means to them. Here is an authentic depiction of Piney culture from those who proudly proclaim themselves New Jersey's Pineys. 144 pages, paperback. ISBN: 978-1-947889-24-8. $22.95

Seasons in the Pine Barrens
Miriam S. Moss

"I spent years observing the natural world in New Jersey's Pine Barrens and recording my thoughts. From the 1970s to the 1990s my husband Sidney and I spent weekends in our primitive cabin. This book represents thoughts generated by quietly sitting in this cabin observing life and nature in the world of my time. These entries still speak to my deepest feelings, now at age 92, much as they did decades ago. My hope is that these words will also be meaningful to you." 196 pages, paperback ISBN: 978-1-947889-15-6. $26.00

Seasons
Dallas Lore Sharp

"Nature appears at her best when Dallas Lore Sharp introduces it." So wrote an anonymous book reviewer in the *Journal of Education* in August 1912 about the author of *Seasons*. Born in 1870 in Haleyville, Sharp spent his childhood roaming the woods beside the Cohansey and Maurice Rivers. He went on to become one of the most popular nature writers of his day, whose essays appeared in the *Atlantic Monthly*, *Harpers*, and *Century*. A "rare and honest soul," he sought to inspire young people to share his appreciation for the glories of the natural world available in their own backyards. Whether his subject is a family of owls who live in a gnarled old apple tree or the common toad he observed for several seasons, Sharp writes with near-mystic appreciation for the most commonplace flora and fauna. *Seasons* presents a selection of essays first published in Sharp's *The Whole Year Round*. With a new foreword by Renee Fern. 158 pages, paperback. ISBN: 978-0-9888731-1-7. $14.95

The Nature of Things
Dallas Lore Sharp

Our second volume of engaging essays from Dallas Lore Sharp's *The Whole Year Round* (originally published in 1915). Sharp, born in 1870 in Haleyville, Cumberland County, New Jersey, was an outstanding essayist writing for young adults in the early twentieth century. 179 pages, paperback. ISBN: 978-1-947889-00-2. $14.95

Everyday Adventures
Samuel Scoville Jr.

Everyday Adventures includes twelve essays that describe Samuel Scoville Jr.'s jaunts into nature with arresting detail. The essays introduce readers to hibernating mammals, snakes, and orchids. But perhaps the most evident animals mentioned are birds. Whether listening to birdsong, searching for hidden nests (which remain undisturbed), or quietly observing avian daily routines, Scoville describes his surroundings vividly and often with considerable wit. He recounts expeditions in Connecticut, the Berkshires, Pennsylvania, Delaware, the Pine Barrens, and the far north of Canada. Quickly, readers find that they have stepped into everyday adventures of their own. 252 pages, paperback. ISBN: 978-0-9976699-9-2. $14.95

The Out of Doors Club
Samuel Scoville Jr.

A collection of essays that follows the adventures of the "Band," a group of young siblings led on imagination-filled hikes by their father. In twenty brief essays, many set in the Pine Barrens, Samuel Scoville Jr. reminds readers of simpler times, when the world held fewer cares and walking in nature could be the highlight of a day. Trekking through fields, bogs and forests, canoeing down rivers, the Band learn amusing lessons about nature and life. Readers will appreciate the gentle and loving relationship depicted between father, mother, and children. 147 pages, paperback. ISBN: 978-1-947889-90-3. $14.95

Swan Bay Jim & Gasoline Seventeen Cents a Gallon; Moonshine a Dollar a Quart
Gary B. Giberson

The mayor of Port Republic for over three decades, Gary B. Giberson is a master decoy-carver, entrepreneur and author. This volume pairs two short stories with illustrations from distinguished artist Kathy Anne English. Follow a poignant hunt through the cedar swamps of the Mullica River and join an adventurous chase to capture rum runners during Prohibition. Photographs courtesy of Gary Giberson. Illustrations by Kathy Anne English. 40 pages, paperback. ISBN: 978-0-9976699-4-7. $7.95